GEMMA MORGAN is an inspiring keynote speaker and leadership consultant with over 25 years' experience across the military, business and elite sport. The founder of Morgan Eight Ltd, she is called upon for expert opinions on a range of subjects including women in leadership, resilience, and what it takes to build a high-performing team. Gemma began her career as an Army Officer and was the first woman to be awarded the Carmen Sword from HRH Princess Royal. She was Captain of the Wales lacrosse team, gaining 85 caps and ranked the 'Most Valuable player in Europe' at the 1997 European Championships. Gemma took part in a BBC TV documentary about Gareth Malone and the Invictus Games Choir and in 2023 her story featured in the 'Road to Recovery' Exhibition at the National Army Museum, London. Gemma campaigns for mental health awareness and is an ambassador for the charity Help for Heroes.

www.gemma-morgan.com

'Read this and talk to your loved ones. Perhaps Gemma's greatest service to her country will be in sharing her story, in the hope that future generations do not suffer the same trauma. While the horrors of war will always create casualties, it is the betrayal by her military bosses which stands out as the deeper wound.'

*Lieutenant-Colonel (Retd) D**⋯⋯* *A**⋯⋯* *O**⋯⋯*

GW00500189

Praise for the author

'Gemma's writing is a shocking read, exposing the British Army as brutal, misogynist and abusive; devoid of the very principles and ethics it demands its soldiers to uphold. This is a wake-up call.'
Paula Edwards, CEO, Salute Her UK

Gemma's story is heart-rending, brutal and at times difficult to stomach. The pathologising of her suffering by military leaders has had devastating consequences. Against all odds she has survived and now demonstrates the very best of what it means to serve and protect the freedoms of others. Written with true courage, *Pink Camouflage* gives hope to all those in our UK Armed Forces who seek justice. They deserve better than this.
Mandy Bostwick, Specialist Trauma Psychotherapist

'Every time I hear her story, it stops me in my tracks. It is visceral, unnerving and spine tingling. It is also one of hope – great big floodlights of hope. But I don't have to tell you this, now you can read it for yourself. Thank you for your service Gemma.'
Antony Cotton MBE, actor and patron of Help for Heroes

'Gemma inspires with powerful vulnerability. She challenges what is means to be a strong leader and has taught me a great deal about finding resilience even in the toughest of times.'
Gareth Malone OBE, choirmaster and broadcaster

Pink Camouflage

One soldier's story
from trauma and abuse to
resilience and leadership

GEMMA MORGAN

Luath Press Limited
EDINBURGH
www.luath.co.uk

First published 2024

ISBN: 978-1-80425-123-2

The paper used in this book is recyclable. It is made
from low chlorine pulps produced in a low energy,
low emission manner from renewable forests.

Printed and bound by
Robertson Printers, Forfar

Typeset in 11.5 point Sabon LT by
Main Point Books, Edinburgh

Contents

To the loves of my life:

Beth, Tom and James
who continue to make me so proud,
you are my reasons for being,

and David,
my rock amidst the chaos,
thank you for standing by me
even when I tried to push you away.

Foreword

RIGHT FROM THE start of this book there is a sense of disbelief and incredulity that this must be a work of fiction and that there has been a very liberal dose of journalistic licence. However, this story is searingly true and cuts right to the heart of life for a female soldier in today's Army. It is a hard-hitting, graphic, honest and, at times, brutal recount of a promising career tainted with misogyny, trauma and, at the end, betrayal. Gemma Morgan is one of the lucky ones who has survived all kinds of hell to tell her story, in an effort to inspire the many others that are now battling to acclimatise to civilian life.

My son, Christopher, died aged 35, as a result of PTSD from his army service. Like Gemma, Chris was also a Captain, trained at the revered Sandhurst Academy. Upon discharge he suffered similar mental health challenges and expressed so many of the same feelings. It makes you think – does the Army really take care of its own? *Pink Camouflage* is a fascinating insight into a macho, male-dominated world where reality is so grotesquely distorted from the public perception. Read it, believe it, because sometimes the truth is far more incredible than fiction.

Terry Butcher
former captain of the England football
team, author of *Bloodied But Unbowed*

Dear Reader,

Checking in to a mental health hospital wasn't part of the plan. This book wasn't either. I spent years in hiding trying to maintain the façade, after all I believed it was my fault; I accepted that something was fundamentally wrong with me.

I began writing as a form of therapy, trying to make sense of it all. For years, the pages sat locked in a secret drawer because I still felt a deep loyalty to the British Army. Then I read the recent cases of Officer Cadet Olivia Perks, Royal Artillery Gunner Jaysley Becks and the hundreds of testimonials from serving women in the Atherton Report.* The Army says that it has made changes and that mine is a historical case. Recent evidence strongly suggests that there has been little meaningful change.

And so, I feel it is my duty to share my story with you. I've included some of the most heart-rendering, positive and painful moments of my life. Whilst some names and personal information have been changed to preserve anonymity, I have battled to describe my experience with unfiltered honesty.

Staying silent nearly killed me. Now, for the first time, this is my whole truth. I hope that it may give strength to anyone else who is suffering. It is for you and for those that love you that I have found my voice. This is me and for that I make no apology.

Take care, love, Gem

* The Defence Sub-Committee on Women in the Armed Forces report *Protecting Those Who Protect Us: Women in the Armed Forces from Recruitment to Civilian Life.* 25 July 2021.

Introduction

HE FOUND ME by the roadside, delirious and choking. I was 33, happily married with two beautiful young children, a poster girl for female achievement with a stellar Army service record and a glittering international sports career.

But behind this golden public image, I was a wreck.

The British Army had taught me to achieve more than I ever thought I could – but it was a lesson that came at a price. The reality of the Army's quest for gender equality meant moulding – forcing – female recruits to fit masculine ideals. Desperate to be part of the team, I tried to camouflage my femininity, to crush and slowly dismantle my identity.

The Army's toxic culture – the sexual abuse and misogyny – prepared the ground for the nightmares long before I saw the man lying dead in the snow in pools of bright red, frozen blood. The sexism of life in barracks undermined me long before I saw the shreds of flesh hanging off shattered limbs and the soulless dark brown eyes. I was a soldier, but contrary to everything I had been led to believe, I found myself powerless to alleviate the suffering all around me.

When I was deployed on a highly unusual operation as a soldier out of uniform with no military back-up, not even a satellite phone, the Army neither offered me guidance, nor asked how I was faring. When I came back to Britain, they never asked what it was like to be an unarmed soldier in civilian clothing deployed in the middle of the blood and mayhem.

I left the Army on my own accord. I ran away, hoping the nightmares would stop. There was no medical discharge. One minute you were in. The next you were gone. My new identity ripped from me. The nightmares replayed again and again in my head. I could not unsee what I had seen.

Then a grenade was thrown into the mix. I gave birth to a baby girl. Motherhood left me lost and alienated. I was a soldier who had no idea how to be a mother. The Army had stolen my femininity. Behind closed doors, vodka, Valium and sleeping pills numbed the pain. Panic distorted the world. It left me isolated and alone. I was constantly on my guard, checking behind me, scanning every window, every corner. I stopped answering the phone and hid when the doorbell rang. I walked with a look designed to make someone think twice. I was more like a bodyguard than a mother.

I found myself drowning, gasping for any pocket of air. In the room, but not really present, not part of the world. Parts of me began to shut down. There was no-one to turn to. The ties with my military family had been cut. Back in the day, there was no help from charities like Help for Heroes – they didn't yet exist. The NHS doctors I saw seemed baffled and confused. Then after seven years of hiding, I hit a rock bottom that led me to that desolate roadside.

In 2006, I was diagnosed with severe Post-Traumatic Stress Disorder. At first, it brought a feeling of intense relief. It was vindication after years of being ignored. Years of thinking that I was at fault. Identifying behind four letters – PTSD – made living easier. It stopped the questions and offered an explanation. I used it to artic-ulate who I was, what I was not and why my suffering and illness were somehow valid.

But as the years passed, I began to wonder how such a short period of time had left such a lasting impact on me. I was in the Army for less than seven years. It was a drop in the ocean, but the ripples of trauma have travelled with me and seeped into each and every part of my life. It has infected those I love and it has destroyed those that I have loved. But I have also been blessed. With the support of my family and the profes-sional help of doctors and therapists I have been able to rebuild my life.

In Narrative Therapy in 2007 we were told to write down our life story. It helped me, but I hated sharing what I had written. This book grew out of that first session. Fear gripped me as I began to write. Each word challenged my urge to remain invisible, to hide. I stopped and put the manuscript away in a drawer time and time again, but it kept calling me back, pushing me to confront who I really am, to make sense of things for myself, on my own. I had to tell this story for the thousands of other women who have been harmed by the toxic culture that pervades the British Army. It is not the trauma that steals so many lives. It is the shame and guilt. This book has been an exorcism: I refuse to entertain this devil into my 50s.

Gemma Morgan
February 2024

I

Serve to Lead

IN JANUARY 1996, I climbed the great white steps of the Royal Military Academy Sandhurst, ironing board tucked under my arm. I was 22 and it was the first day of Army Officer Training. I would not walk up the steps of Old College again until our commissioning parade 11 months later.

I had just driven past the guard at the Staff College Gate and along the mile-long driveway through the woods and past the Upper Lake. I felt excited, but I had no idea what was about to come. I parked in front of Old College – the only time I would be allowed to. The main parade ground stretched out in front of the building. I would spend the first term there with the other male and female cadets.

The sense of history was unmistakeable. Pillars topped by a pediment displaying the cipher of George III and supported on each side by figures of Mars and Minerva, the gods of war and wisdom, led you to the door. Cannons from Waterloo guarded the front and the square was flanked by guns from the 18th century and the Crimean War.

Entering the two huge black doors of the Grand

Entrance revealed walls covered with antique weapons, silverware and pictures. Stained glass windows in the Indian Army Memorial Room record the close links between the British and Indian Armies down to 1948, with the corridor walls showcasing grand relics of the colonial past. I was met by the Directing Staff who swiftly ushered me off to my accommodation. No first names. From now on I was Officer Cadet Lowth.

My parents had no idea why I had joined up. As a child I had never expressed any interest in being a soldier. There was no proud family military tradition and I had gone to an all-girls school where there was no organisation such as the cadets. I had a friend who had joined the Army and, spurred on by a TV campaign which showed soldiers skiing and jumping out of planes, I decided to join her. It was not necessarily the lifestyle that drew me in; after all, I knew nothing about military life. It was more the boredom of everything else. I craved to escape the graduate 'milk-round' and do something truly meaningful with my life.

Walking through the enclave of Sandhurst, I felt the excitement of breaking the rules. I was stepping over the patriarchal line. I was one of the few women to do the same training as the men. Female platoons were still kept separate and only a handful of roles were open to women, but the message was all about empowerment, that girls could have it all. The reality was that in becoming a female soldier I also became an immediate outlier within the very institution I had joined.

I was a middle-class girl from Surrey. I had been brought up to believe that women should have the same opportunities as men. My parents gave my brother, two sisters and I every opportunity. I was the 'sporty one'. Dad stood on the side-lines of every training session and at each fixture he was there to support me. After a game, we would dissect my performance on the way home. I captained the England under-18s lacrosse side and won a place to study Sport and Exercise Science at the University of Birmingham. After graduating, I started a postgraduate teacher training course for Secondary English and PE. I was inspired by my sports teacher and I decided to follow in her footsteps, but three quarters of the way through I realised it was not for me. Teaching felt more like policing. I was looking for something more.

It was not just the seductive message of female empowerment that brought me to Sandhurst. I was drawn by the Army's promise of belonging and the idea of service. I joined up, as many of us did, believing that the Army would offer a career with value and meaning. It was well intentioned. I was seeking connection, purpose and belonging. It felt like an adventure.

I had my first taste of leadership as captain of the school lacrosse team. Back then, leading was all about being captain – a given rank, if you like. As I understood it, being captain was about being the best player. I learned to work harder, to train harder, to get faster and stronger. I developed a fierce work ethic and an insatiable, perfectionist drive. I loved the attention that my achievements brought – the awards, the goals, the newspaper articles – and soon became excessively eager to please. Success meant adulation. It made me feel valued and needed. When I first pulled on an England shirt, I remember the look in Dad's eyes. The pride and excitement were things that we shared together, special moments that would stand the test of time. At home there was no prize for second best.

When I was a child, it never occurred to me that people expected less of me because I was a girl. Being a girl never limited me. I never understood the boundaries, to the amusement and more often frustration of my teachers and parents. I had always been unconventional, challenging the path laid out for me. I played football and outperformed many of the boys, but I was restricted to the garden or park as girls were not allowed in the clubs back then. In swimming lessons, I was determined to wear the same as the boys and persisted each week in a pair of trunks. I saw no reason to squeeze into a restrictive costume or, worse still, a flimsy bikini. I wanted to swim unrestricted, to run, climb and wrestle in the mud. Dad joked that I should have been born a boy. Looking back, it would have been a whole lot easier.

Every Sunday, Sandhurst cadets went to church in the redbrick Memorial Chapel in the middle of Chapel Square, which is framed by pretty Georgian houses. It is a peaceful spot, full of reflection and memory. Solemn but beautiful, it was a place where you could close your eyes and breathe for a moment.

The main entrance faces a bronze statue dedicated to the soldiers who died in both World Wars: a reminder of the close link between officers and other ranks, that we are there to serve them as well as our country. Inside, the names of the fallen of 1914–1918 are recorded on the white marble pillars. A book of remembrance records the names of all officers of Commonwealth armies who died in the Second World War. In the chapel sanctuary there is another book for the years since 1945. A cadet turns the page every Sunday. High up on the walls, small stained glass windows display the coats of arms of all deceased Field Marshals appointed since 1939. The words of Matthew 20:28 are inscribed high above the entrance on the interior wall echoing the Sandhurst motto, 'Serve to Lead'. I looked up and read it silently every time I filed out of the building:

> For even the Son of Man came not to be served but to serve others and to give his life as a ransom for many.

Sandhurst transformed me. It turned my understanding of leadership on its head. The motto is emblazoned on every lectern, every cap badge and in every hall. The leadership here was profoundly different to the model I had absorbed at school. At Sandhurst, effective leadership did not pivot around time served. It was never about being the top goal-scorer or the best technical specialist. I began to understand the importance of investing in my knowledge and building a presence and credibility where others had confidence in me, but the heartbeat of my transformation came from a realisation that leadership is a choice of service. With the focus switching firmly from me to everyone else, I understood that I had a duty to create an environment where others could thrive. I took seriously the need to set the example, to eat, live and breathe the non-negotiable values at the heart of Army life.

We were constantly pushing for performance perfection. The Directing Staff would drive us unrelentingly towards the limits of what we thought was physically or psychologically possible. They would roar at us whenever we failed to conduct ourselves with the required sense of urgency. Shouting was an accepted form of communication – it was what people did to get their point across. We became accustomed to the raw feedback that would hit you between the eyes. Everything was executed at 'the speed of a thousand gazelles'. Discipline and integrity were non-negotiable. I soon learned the importance of a fastidious attention to detail and an unrelenting daily routine that would form the bedrock of my life.

My behaviours changed. Training taught me to push myself beyond my physical and mental limits. I became a little less human – a tougher, rougher version of myself. I was pleased with the results. The priority was always action. As a cadet you had to walk or run everywhere with a sense of purpose and urgency known as 'cutting about'. We were taught a polarity of thinking, clearly defined and dualistic. Our role was to seek clarity and control, to analyse the problem and – most importantly of all – fix it.

It was about getting better together, with little regard for precious feelings or the comfortable niceties of life. Training was designed to break you down, learning through pain and fear. Hitting the required standard would allow you to breathe for a moment while failure brought more pain. We were forever on edge, ready to spark on command. I learned to exist constantly primed. There were regular 'change parades', where you were forced to change uniforms in 'quick-time' over and over again, as a punishment if someone had been late or not tidied their room properly. We wore the same green boiler suit for the first five weeks – as an Officer Cadet you were ranked below the Staff Sergeant's Labrador. There was the persistent threat of being 'back-termed' and having to start all over again. It was controlling, coercive and at times threatening, yet it also formed some of the best memories of my life. For the first time, I understood what being part of a high-performing team really meant. We did not necessarily all like each other, but we pulled together with a strong bond because the instructors created an environment where we really needed each other, where we depended upon one another to survive.

The first cohort of women to be trained alongside the men had entered Sandhurst just four years earlier. The only allowance made in recognition that women might be different from men was that we carried less weight. Army training set out to impose military masculinity, transforming each of us into a soldier capable of the aggression, risk-taking and violence that was necessary. Physical fitness, overt heterosexuality, emotional control, self-discipline and self-reliance were all central components of the regime. Priority was given to physical conditioning, but the methods were archaic. I had just completed a degree in sport and exercise science – but I knew better than to question the efficiency of what we were doing and why. The Physical Training Instructors were set in their ways and believed that everyone should be subjected to the same kind of nonsense they dealt with as young soldiers. Beastings, repetitive physical exercises dished out as punishment with no defined end point, in hard military boots were viewed as a rite of passage. Reporting an injury was a mark of shame – an excuse to get out of training. You would quickly be labelled 'sick, lame and lazy' and cast aside. Bright pink ibuprofen tablets were dished out daily as the answer to every ailment or injury. We were told to 'suck it up' and 'no pain, no gain' was the favourite rallying cry.

I was lucky – my physical strength meant that I could hold my own amongst the men and comfortably meet the fitness standards required. I could keep the pace. I could set the pace. I could leave many of the men behind. But what my talent gave me with one hand could easily be taken away with the other. At Sandhurst, cadets underwent regular individual fitness tests. Women competed against the men. In the Commandant's Test, an 8-mile run carrying full webbing and weapons followed by an assault course, I finished in the top third. I was congratulated, but the men behind me were publicly shamed as their names were written in white chalk on the blackboard. As a woman, you were damned if you did and damned if you did not. I quickly learned to excel, but not too far, for fear of stepping over the line. I learned how to make myself smaller as I walked into a room in order to survive.

I was given leave to attend an England lacrosse

training squad selection. I was fitter than ever and held my own alongside the best players in the country. In a debrief team meeting I spoke up assertively as I had been taught to do at Sandhurst. The room full of women fell silent. I was too direct and abrupt. The coach took me aside. Her words crushed me. What I heard was that I was technically good enough, but I did not fit in. My behaviour was deemed too challenging. Such a short conversation and yet I was devastated. As a young girl, playing for England was everything I had dreamed of, but now I was excluded. I returned to Sandhurst that evening deflated.

Not long after, Wales invited me to trials for their team. I went to the World Cup in Japan in 1997 playing for my new country. Later that year, I was awarded the 'Most Valuable Player' of the tournament at the European Championships. I would go on to Captain Wales and win 85 international caps. As I walked on stage to collect the trophy, I had two fingers silently raised at my doubters. I became defiant – torching the past to clear the way.

As one of few women at Sandhurst, eyes were on me all the time. Of the 300 cadets in the junior term, about 10 per cent were women. I knew I had to fit in. I became accustomed to a hyper-masculine environment and assumed the expected behaviours. It mattered, as the team was at the heart of everything. There was no mentoring for women, we simply had to be one of the boys. There were so few of us that it became a 'dog-eat-dog' environment. Being the minority in a hyper-masculine culture often meant denying help to those of 'your kind'. As a result, I had only a tiny handful of female friends and I drew back from sharing my thoughts and emotions with 'the girls'. In terms of female officers, there were few role models. Our female Platoon Commander would turn up on exercise wearing makeup and earrings, telling us about her blueberry shower gel from The Body Shop, whilst the rest of us were lying in a trench soaking wet and stinking. She had not actually completed this course alongside the men, but the previous course for women only that existed before.

No-one ever writes it down or verbalises it, but it was clear that I would need to perform to a much higher standard to succeed. I had to work harder, run faster. Inevitably, I became more masculine, my tone became more assertive and direct, my presence more commanding and aggressive. There were no heels or makeup, I chose my clothes to blend in. I began cursing profanities mid-sentence with my peers. We understood that emotion and femininity were signs of weakness. I did not want to be the girl in the Army that looked weak, because they already thought that you were weak. I was constantly fighting not to be 'othered' and I forced my curvier peg into the Army's square hole. I did not want to be one of those girls on the parade square with the high-pitched squeal. Throughout my career I believed that if I was tough then I would be safe. I believed that if I was strong, then they would not treat me as second-rate.

The Army is expert in creating togetherness through hardship, shared goals and a unifying sense of organ-

isation and identity. It is a whole lifestyle and all consuming. There is always somewhere to be and always
a time to be there, no matter what day of the week.
There is no differentiation between work and home – it
is what gives purpose to Army life. An exclusive kind
of camaraderie is instilled to harness team bonding.
Everything is based on the people around you. We
grew to elevate the specialness of our group, treading
down others supposedly less worthy on the outside.

From the first weeks in training they engrain in you
contempt for civilians, changing the way you think
about yourself. I learned to define myself against the
civilian population from which I was drawn – believing
that I was now tougher, stronger and more organised. I
immersed myself in the hype, revelling in the idea that
'civvies' would rely on me. Most of us embraced the
notion that civilians were now slipshod and slovenly and
that we were somehow superior and more disciplined. I
relished this carefully constructed identity – the warrior-
protector archetype.

Life behind the Academy walls was cut off from
the world outside. The IRA threat at the time meant
that we had to hide our military identity. We were not
permitted to walk out of the Academy in uniform or
display any clues in our vehicles. On nights out someone
was assigned 'shark watch', meaning that they would
stay sober and alert to the environment. It meant that
we were very much out of sight and out of mind to
civilian communities. We were effectively cut off from
normal life.

Belonging became a powerful uniting force, but it

was strictly conditional. The staff set themselves up as a kind of enemy, making it clear that the weak and idle were a liability. They moulded each one of us into a vision of what they wanted us to be and how they wanted us to behave. There became this contagious drive to jettison the weak and banish the 'biffs'. Those who are sick or injured are issued a sick chit by their unit medic, otherwise known as a biff chit. Biff is slang for those deemed less capable. It is a disparaging term that is usually preceded by a series of expletives. On the parade ground the biffs were singled out and had to stand at the back of their platoon. They were ridiculed. I learned to hide any sense of vulnerability, to maintain this veneer of defiant perfection at all times. The team was all that mattered, with no space given for indulgent 'navel-gazing'. Shaming those who dared to deviate served to galvanise our unity. I was fine with that; it felt like a rite of passage.

During the first term at Sandhurst, I struggled for a few days with my health. I kept feeling lightheaded and fainting. One night I had to stay in the medical centre. The blood tests showed an elevated white count. First day back on parade the Sergeant Major asked if congratulations were in order and whether he needed to knit blue or pink for the imminent arrival. He hauled me out in front of everyone, thinking he was hilarious. We had to write a journal and submit it to the Platoon Commander each week. I wrote about the incident and conveyed my humiliation, only to be summoned to her office, warned to 'wind my neck in' and not dare to be so insolent.

At the end of the year, after 44 weeks of training, it was time for the Sovereign's Parade. After the two-hour parade in front of dignitaries, royals, friends and family, we marched off the square for the last time to 'Auld Lang Syne'. As tradition dictates, we were followed by the Adjutant riding his white charger up the steps immediately behind us. Passing through the portals of the Grand Entrance of Old College at your Sovereign's Parade is meant to represent the beginning of a professional British Army Officer's career. It was largely lost on me. My fingers and toes were frozen in the December cold. I just remember feeling an overwhelming sense of relief. I could not wait to get started.

I officially became an officer at midnight during the Commissioning Ball. I wore my regimental mess dress for the first time. It was dark navy-blue, with a black cropped jacket finished with gold trimming. As the midnight hour struck, fireworks lit up the sky and my sisters removed the tape from my shoulder straps, revealing the single 'pips' that denoted my new rank of Second Lieutenant.

2

The Brotherhood

THE ARMY ENTICED us with a promise of brotherhood. When I graduated from Sandhurst, I believed I was joining a family united by powerful ideals of loyalty, honour, integrity, duty, sacrifice and courage. The Army had sold itself as a world set apart from – and superior to – the normality of civilian life. It instilled in me a drive to 'Be the Best', calling me to earn my place in this special group.

Although parts of the establishment doubled down on the masculine ideal, it did not seem like gender bias at the time. I tolerated it because I was so immersed in army life. I loved what the Army stood for and the people I served with. The last thing I wanted was to be 'othered'. It is hard to stay in 'the club' if you speak out against it.

The pace was incessant, but I had never felt more alive. The Army taught me that I could achieve more than I had ever imagined. I still miss being a sister in the brotherhood, the connection, the banter, the military language, the adrenaline, the discipline and focus. But I will never miss wearing men's combat boots in a smaller size, because they did not make kit for women, or wearing a uniform that cut across my boobs and thighs. I am glad to be rid of the Army's less palatable side, of the misogyny and the abuse.

After Sandhurst, I was posted to the Royal Logistic Corps 60 Transport Squadron at Dalton Barracks in Abingdon. I was a Troop Commander responsible for 45 soldiers and millions of pounds worth of equipment. Our primary role was to supply ammunition to the Royal Artillery. It was more complicated than it sounds, as the handling and storage of high explosives and ammunition require strict safety procedures. In the modern Army, it involves far more than just moving bullets about.

A Troop Commander is one of the best jobs in the Army because it involves every aspect of a soldier's life. I was debt advisor, career manager and leader for some incredible young men and women. It is a job that really makes a difference when you get it right. I was lucky to have a supportive Sergeant and Staff Sergeant to guide me.

At Christmas there was a drinks party with officers at the Sergeants' Mess. As I was leaving, a senior soldier approached me. He forced me into a small closet where there was a payphone. His breath stank. His hands lunged at me. He was aggressive and domineering. He was a tall man and much stronger than me. He had served over 15 years, and I was just a young lieutenant on my first posting. He pushed up against me. I could feel him. He kept holding my face and chin. The phone booth smelt of stale cigarettes. His other hand propped up on the wall above me. I tried to appease him, grimacing, as polite as I could be. We were in a public place and the noise from the bar seemed to disturb him. He recoiled and let me go. The next thing I knew I was on the road between the Sergeants' and the Officers' Mess trying not to run as the panic built up inside me. I can still hear the sound of my boots on the tarmac. I had no idea who to turn to or who would help me. There was nothing I could do. That is the way it works – by isolation and intimidation. I said nothing.

One night when I was on guard duty, he refused to hand over the duty file when I texted him. He told me to come and collect it at his house, adding his wife was out. His behaviour was controlling and threatening. I felt tense and alert moving around the barracks, anticipating where he might be in case I bumped into him.

Uninvited groping was commonplace at the bar or under the table at formal dinners. Groups of men would run scorecards with names of nightly conquests listed down the side; the points for a young female officer were some of the highest you could win. One officer's favourite party trick was to 'weigh' your breasts, leaning in to mumble his cheeks against your cleavage for good measure. It was all just accepted as 'banter' – a jovial part of army life in which boys would be boys. For all the talk about discipline and integrity, so many issues were either ignored or brushed away. At Sandhurst, the instructors had slept with other instructors, as well as cadets. You could call it fraternisation, but it was also an abuse of authority. A commissioned male officer let himself into our rooms at night. We would wake to find him standing over our beds in the dark. We made a complaint, but no meaningful action was ever taken against him. It was lesson number one in military life. In Abingdon, soldiers would mount hard-core pornography all over their walls before room inspection. Other officers walked on by, but when I asked for it to be removed, I was laughed at, branded frigid and uptight.

At Sandhurst, I was seeing someone. I was in his bedroom, when I looked up to see his friends watching through the panel of glass above the door. That was the culture – they would tell their male friends so they could come and watch. At Abingdon there was a captain who would boast about positioning the woman from behind so that his mates could come in the room during the act, without her knowledge, and take photos. Your peers were not just your friends. We were all in competition against each other for promotion. If you complained to a superior it could single you out. It created a toxic chain of command where it was easier to stay silent.

They lived by a pack mentality. We were known as 'lumpy jumpers', 'Doris' or 'split arse' in conversations down the lines. It was all a means of expressing power, to make us feel inferior. Similar derogatory terms were used to refer to the foreign cadets. They were called FLOPIES – fucking lazy overseas people. Abuse was the norm and therefore accepted. It was wearing and degrading – the only way to cope was to let it all wash over me. It was fast becoming a fact of life.

Heavy drinking was prescribed, even demanded of you, as a young officer. It was what people did.

Nights out were often disorderly with confusing and contradictory standards on exactly how female officers should behave. I remember being summoned to the Officers' Mess to celebrate a senior officer's promotion. I had an international training camp that weekend, so I ordered a soft drink. I was clearly instructed to 'man up' and to get something stronger down my neck. We were not allowed to leave the bar early. We had to wait until the celebrated commander had left the building. Just after midnight my Officer Commanding announced that there would be physical training at 0600hrs. When the alarm rang at 0530hrs, I could not coordinate my arms and legs to get dressed. I staggered to the hangar where my Staff Sergeant took one look at me and hid me in the centre of the squad. As we started marching, the soldiers to my right and left held me upright, the soldier to the rear kept me moving forwards. When we returned into the hangar, we formed a circle to start stretching. The colour drained from my face and my legs started swaying. I managed to make it to my office before I started vomiting in the waste paper bin. It took me days to recover, but it was all seen as 'good fun'. The drunken scrapes people got into were laughed off as a rite of passage. It earned me more 'points' from the lads, suggesting that I was an officer and teammate worth having.

My room was in the Officers' Mess. It was a large, stately building with long corridors of single accommodation organised in order of seniority. We were brought a cup of tea every morning and a silver service dinner was laid on every night. Alcohol was heavily subsidised.

A shot of vodka cost next to nothing. There were endless formal dinner nights with officers dressed up smartly in full attire. It was the custom for junior officers to stay behind and finish the better quality port left at the top table.

One evening, I left the dinner in the early hours and staggered back to my room along the corridor. I undressed and collapsed on my bed. The room started spinning. It was warm as I drifted off to sleep lying on top of my duvet. I awoke a few hours later, confused and startled. My eyes were stinging, unable to focus clearly. I remember rolling over and retching as my throat burned. My naked body was covered in a corrosive, white substance that stuck to my skin. My room had been broken into by two male officers armed with a dry powder fire extinguisher. They had stood over me whilst I was sleeping and painted my naked body. My room was covered in what looked like a fresh fall of snow. It destroyed my stereo and computer. I was scared and vulnerable. I had no idea what else they might have done to me that night. It left me in a heightened state of anxiety, but I was also angry. I arrived at work later than usual the next morning and was called to see the Commanding Officer. Before he could start to reprimand me, I told him what had happened. I was enraged. He simply smiled, amused by the story. He did nothing about it, although one of the men did see fit to apologise. I said no more. I was drunk, and if you were drunk, it was your fault. We all knew that – but now even my bedroom felt unsafe.

I was left with almost no control over my life. In the

military you cannot simply leave your job at the end of the day and go home. From that moment onwards, I checked I had locked my bedroom door multiple times every night. I took a 'wingman' each and every time I chose to socialise. Some people might call it a game, but for others it is more volatile. Neither home nor work was a safe place to be. I was bound by the rules and trapped behind the wire. Kosovo would be the tipping point for my mental health, but some of the most serious damage had been done to me in barracks during training long before I left for the Balkans.

3

Kosovo

A VICIOUS CONFLICT had erupted in a tiny corner of south-eastern Europe – Kosovo. While it has been superseded by many others, that does not diminish the violence, terror and horrors it unleashed on its citizens.

A political stand-off between the Serbs and the ethnic Albanians who lived in Serbia's southern province had turned violent. In 1995 the Dayton Accords ended the war in Bosnia. Croatia, Bosnia and the rump Federal Republic of Yugoslavia (which consisted of Serbia and Montenegro) all recognised one another. This left Kosovo Albanians, who had until now relied on a policy of passive resistance to achieve their aim of independence, feeling betrayed by the international community. Exiled militants now moved centre stage and shifted their war from Swiss cafés to the mountains of northern Albania. In the spring of 1997, just as they did so, the Albanian state imploded. As the government lost control, the army dissolved and the police ran away. Arms depots were thrown open. Guns and ammunition flooded over the border into Kosovo and into the hands of the Kosovo Liberation Army, the KLA. In the spring of 1998, it emerged from the shadows: a guerrilla war of a type previously unseen in the former Yugoslavia. The Serbian police and the Yugoslav Army retaliated, sending tens of thousands of people fleeing before them. Houses in KLA strongholds were looted and torched. Crops burned and cattle were machine gunned.

After the UN Security Council called for an immediate ceasefire under Resolution 1199 in October 1998, a deal was struck under which Serbian military and police presence was to be brought down to pre-war levels. The Organisation for Security and Co-operation in Europe (OSCE) Kosovo Verification Mission, the KVM, was set up to monitor Serbian and KLA compliance. I was 25 years old and deployed as one of the OSCE monitors. I got the call while I was on a rock-climbing course. I was literally on the rock face. A shot of adrenaline rushed through me. I was filled with excitement and anticipation.

Before I left, I washed and ironed everything. Shoes polished and positioned immaculately in my wardrobe as if ready for inspection. I burned old love letters and binned anything incriminating. The last thing I wanted was for my parents to find something that might make them think less of me. Should the worst happen, I was determined that there would be no skeletons left hanging around for others to find. I filled in the standard army form leaving a simple note for loved ones and sealed the brown envelope. I then sat down to write a private letter to my parents. They had never understood why I had joined up and my mother had become anxious from the moment she found out I was being sent to Kosovo. My words were considered and heartfelt, yet I hoped that they would never have cause to be read.

We were put on standby and gathered at the Army base in South Cerney to prepare. We were trained on how to use an interpreter and briefed on the basics of the situation in Kosovo. Medics taught us advanced first aid and we experimented on ourselves with needles and IV infusions. At first, I thought it was because I was one of the most junior officers to have been selected that I found my questions going unanswered. Everything was chaotic and uncertain. When one of the senior officers decided that he would rather not go and explained to me that we were all volunteers and this was not a conventional deployment, I began to realise that there was no game plan. No-one knew exactly what was happening on the ground or what we were actually going to do when we got there, let alone where we would live and what we would eat.

I knew virtually nothing about Kosovo. I knew more about Bosnia. Like everyone else, I had seen the headlines and watched the news. At a military level, I expected Kosovo would be like Bosnia and that I would be in a military environment on peace-keeping patrols. How little I knew.

One morning we were told that a press conference was going to be held in one of the hangars. The journalists all wanted to talk to me, as I was one of three women to join the mission. I enjoyed talking to the reporter from *The Times*, but the tabloid reporters were completely different. They wanted 'to pink it and shrink it'. The line of questioning singled me out as vulnerable, as if I was unequal to my male counterparts. What was it like to be a woman in this environment? Did I have any concerns? What about family at home? How would I cope with little sanitary provision? How would I feel living confined with the men? The line of questioning was insulting. I became increasingly irritated and progressively evasive. They probed on seemingly unaware of the offence they were causing.

Days later, when the Ministry of Defence issued a press release which simply said that a handful of military personnel were going to advise the KVM, I was already on my way to Kosovo with 134 British military personnel. We were dressed in civilian clothes and carrying diplomatic passports.

We were taken to a hotel in Brezovica, high up in mountains by the Macedonian border. Brezovica had once been one of the most popular ski resorts in the former Yugoslavia. Now it was deserted. The tourists had gone. On the lamp-posts and trees, missing person posters were fraying in the wind. The Americans had already initiated a well-established operation called the Kosovo Diplomatic Observer Mission, KDOM, for several months before we arrived and their staff ran a series of introductory briefings on human rights and humanitarian issues.

The atmosphere was confusing. As we were all in civilian clothes, it was impossible to tell people's rank. It was clear it was best not to ask too many questions. It was a strange, bizarre world where I never even knew the surnames of many of my colleagues.

While waiting to receive further instructions, I noticed a short, portly man wearing a ski jacket being escorted inside. It was Major General John Drewienkiewicz, who headed up the British element of the mission. Out of uniform he seemed smaller and grandfatherly. He asked to speak with me and took me for a walk to discuss his proposition. He needed a 'Miss Moneypenny' to work with the head of the KVM, the American diplomat William Walker. Why was he asking me and not one of the many capable male officers? I was told he needed 'a female who would look after his diary and have a calming presence in the office.' You see it everywhere – women being cherry-picked to take administrative roles, even if they are trained in another field. My heart sank. There was no discussion. We left for Pristina (Prishtina in Albanian), the capital of Kosovo, two days later.

We drove into Pristina in a civilian car past the Serbian checkpoints. The snow had melted on the pavements and turned into a dirty slush. Mist hung in the air. Everything was covered in black grime. Even the air felt unclean. From the car window, I was struck by the piles of rubbish and the wild dogs rifling through the bins.

I was dropped at the 'Hotel Grand', a misnamed, 13-storey block of socialist era concrete that was buzzing with journalists and soldiers. When the Grand opened in 1978, it had at least tried to live up to its name, but by 1998 the brown rooms, brown tap water and lumpy food gave it a down-at-heel feel that was compounded by the suspicious looking staff and the track-suited gangsters in the lobby.

I naively tipped the porter half his monthly wage

as he carried my suitcases into the room. I lay down on the bed to take stock. I decided it would be a good idea to run a bath. I had just eased into the warmth of the water when machine gun fire exploded in the street below. I hit the floor to take cover, my heart racing, ready to flee. Naked and prone on all fours, a family of cockroaches scuttled across my right hand.

Soon the gunfire would barely register. I learned to differentiate between the whizz and crack of bullets heading in my direction and those just playing away from me across the street. My commute to work consisted of walking across a couple of blocks, always alone and exposed on the silent streets. Rubbish festered on every corner. At first I held my breath – the putrid stench was gagging – but I grew accustomed to the sights and smells. I learned to accept the filth and the chaos, the tension and the lies. I learned not to trust anyone or to rely on anything.

William Walker completely ignored me. I was given an office at the other end of the building from his. Then, I was given the wrong timings for external meetings or press briefings. I sat for weeks doing nothing meaningful and my time in post started to grate. While other nations merged KDOM observers into the KVM, America did not. Their KDOM people were supplied by DynCorp, a US company based in Virginia. Most of the people that work for it are former members of US military elite units or the CIA. They are under contract to the State Department and so when the CIA needs to put people into places but not be seen to be involved, it turns to DynCorp or its competitors. Needless to say, they had a wide-ranging interpretation of the brief. It was quickly very clear that there had never been a role for me, other than to serve as a pair of British eyes in the American camp. I was shocked by the political rivalry and infighting. Disillusioned, I spent days on my computer surfing the internet and updating my CV. Turf wars compounded the chaos and the duplicity.

Then masked gunmen burst into the Panda café in Peć (known as Peja by Albanians) and gunned down six teenagers playing pool. It has never been established precisely who carried out the attack, but 5,000 angry and frightened Serbs turned up to their funerals.

Although Kosovo Serbs were also victims of KLA violations of humanitarian law, there was nothing close to a tit for tat. Serbian strategy was well rehearsed and brutally implemented. There were mass forced expulsions, often accompanied by the deliberate destruction of property and looting.

I called home just before Christmas. It was my sister's 21st birthday and they were having a big party to celebrate. I did not say much and must have sounded rather distant as I knew the Serbs were listening – you could hear the faint clicking on the line. There was a strange pull to hear my family's voices, yet it made emotions bubble up to the surface that I could not allow myself to show.

One day I'd had enough. I marched down the corridor towards General Drewienkiewicz's office. My anger propelled me past the Colonel sitting outside. I announced myself and the General looked up from behind his desk with a rather bemused smile. He said

I had balls to march in like that and agreed to a new deployment. As I walked out of the General's office, the Colonel looked up, unimpressed. I told him that I didn't want to spend my whole tour behind a desk. He replied that he had got the message, suggesting I should consider why I had joined up as an officer in the first place. I didn't care what he thought about me – I was out of there and hoping for better things.

4

Daisy Chains

I ARRIVED IN Peć on Christmas Eve. It is a historic city in one of the most beautiful corners of Kosovo, surrounded by the mountains that form the border with Montenegro. It was completely different from Pristina. The air was fresh and the snow was crisp and clean. Peć was once an important stopping point on the vital trading route between Constantinople, as Istanbul used to be known, and Dubrovnik on the Adriatic. Many of the buildings had been torched, but its ancient bazaar remained intact. There were still restaurants and cafés.

Peć had a mixed population and the situation in the city was tense. More than any other part of Kosovo, Peć holds a spiritual significance for Serbs as it has been the seat of the Serbian Orthodox Patriarchate since the 13th century. Serbs regard it as the cultural cradle of their nation. Added to this explosive mix was the presence of a small number of Serbs in the surrounding villages who had already been expelled or fled from Croatia. The KLA was in control of the hills to the west and the highlands to the south-east.

The KVM mission was made up of around 30 verifiers and a team of local staff. Many of the men were Americans from DynCorp, while others were serving soldiers from Germany, Canada, Russia, Italy and France. At first, we were all housed together. I was one of two military women. I soon formed a close bond with Ella, the only other woman, who was a Canadian officer. We shared a room and by necessity we looked out for each other. We watched each other's backs, particularly when alcohol was about.

On Christmas Day, Ella and the other Canadian soldiers opened what they called 'care packages' from home, reading messages from people they had never met, but who had written to each of them thanking them for their service. Ella pulled out a huge cigar and sat laughing with it in her mouth by the fire. It seemed surreal and far removed from the way that we did things in the UK. We sat on the rooftop to welcome in the New Year, a beer in one hand and a cigarette in the other, listening to celebratory gunfire rip through the night sky.

I began working as a Fusion Officer in what was known as the Fusion Cell. It was an office where the reports, interviews, photographs and videos supplied by the KVM patrols were collated and studied for intelligence. I also started to go out on KVM monitoring missions to get to know the area and give the monitors some time off.

We would patrol around the country in our bright orange vehicles. The Albanians saw us as a small beacon of hope. Our arrival offered brief moments of safety and respite. To get the information we needed we had to build genuine relationships with people otherwise they were suspicious and refused to talk. We would sit for hours drinking coffee and smoking cigarettes with the villagers by the side of the road and soon they invited us into their homes.

The Albanian villagers called me 'Djamelia'. At the time I thought nothing of the name itself. 'Djamelia' left little impact on me. I presumed that they had misspelled my actual name or adapted it to the cultural setting. I was only told later on about the significance of its meaning to the locals, its association with light and hope.

As we approached in our armoured Humvee, the children would rush out to meet us with smiles that cut through the terror in their lives. Their t-shirts and plastic sandals were out of place in the deep snow and emergency shelters where they had been forced to take refuge. We would emerge from our heated vehicle, dressed in high-tech Salomon jackets and yet they would shout out 'Djamelia' and invite us inside. The women made me gifts of lace doilies; they fed us and welcomed us with warmth and gratitude. The reality was this was the honeymoon period. They had yet to realise that we were powerless to help them, but I already sensed that we were letting them down and failing to keep unspoken promises.

One day I would be drinking coffee with families in their kitchens and the next taking photos of their torched house and dead bodies. It was an anarchy that I could not process. There were no boundaries, no rules or decency, just a lawlessness that pervaded everything. At Sandhurst they had drilled into us a non-negotiable sense of duty – serve to lead. I was already beginning to see that I was failing to meet the values I cherished.

I went out on patrol with Doc, our medic, a few times. Doc was a former US Ranger with a wild gaze and pained smile. He did his own thing and kept to his own rules. He would venture out to visit families he had helped over time. One evening we went for a beer. He leaned over to share something that has stayed with me ever since. He said that if we make a difference to just one person, then we could rest easy that night. Perhaps he wanted to warn me of where the frustration that I was beginning to feel could lead. His words anchored my perspective and rekindled some hope.

In the new year, I began leading a multi-national KVM patrol from south Peć towards Dečan, the home of the famous Visoki Dečani Monastery. It was built in the 14th century by the Serbian King Stefan Dečanski and is his mausoleum. It was a calm bubble where the frenetic world outside was held at bay by the religious serenity. Yet the tranquillity fed my suspicion. The truth is that I did not trust the Serbs. I had lost my neutrality. Anything Serbian was, in my mind, suspect.

I would drive out of Peć and head due south on the almost dead-straight road towards Dečan. To our right were the Accursed Mountains, which formed the border first with Montenegro and then with Albania. I left first thing in the morning and returned home at night. To my left on the way to Dečan was KLA country, villages controlled by one of the biggest Albanian commanders and his brothers. Drive off the main road and you were almost immediately in their territory.

I quickly established a routine. I understood that I needed to build confidence in my leadership and credibility as the team were experienced soldiers, men who had earned their stripes in more testing environments than mine. I learned to clarify expectations and boundaries quickly. The mission was still chaotic and, as people tried to do the right thing, there was a danger of 'mission creep' setting in, where the boundaries of the work start to expand beyond the original brief. The usual controls that would be imposed in a normal military operation were non-existent. Clarifying standard operating procedures was far from easy. In a normal military environment, you have a forward recce to check the route is clear. There was none of that. In a normal military environment, there is a medical evacuation procedure to get you out if you are injured. There was none of that. In a normal British military environment, if your vehicle breaks then they send the Royal Electrical Mechanical Engineers to recover you. There was none of that, no Army for protection. We were on our own.

Each nation had their own view of best practice. Radio discipline was shocking, with many using the net to share anything and everything. One day a fellow patrol was in trouble. We heard 'Contact, Wait Out' called out over the radio. A patrol was taking incoming fire. Most of the time the KLA were just firing warning shots, but everyone else should have stayed silent to allow this patrol commander to speak. The radios are two-way, which means if someone is talking then the other person cannot be heard. However, a different patrol started filling the airwaves with trivia. Agreed standard operating procedures exist to keep everyone safe.

Our Russian colleague did not see the need to check his equipment every morning. He refused to place his field dressing in the same pocket as everyone else and tensions started to rise. Things came to a head when we needed to change a wheel – he refused to let me, a woman, help him. Then there was our French colleague who insisted on his lunch break. His grasp of English was so poor, I re-deployed him as a driver. It was a short-lived move that ended with him refusing to give up his midday glass of wine. Nevertheless, we soon established a regular team and got to grips with the tasks we had in hand.

I was assigned an interpreter called Bashkim. He was in his late 30s. A teacher, Bashkim was married with children. I never found out how many and I never met them, but Bashkim was at my side every day. He was my right-hand man, a light-hearted and joyful character. He lightened the mood. Crucially, I trusted him and felt safe in his company. He treated me as an equal. He was a valued and treasured member of our team.

I wince as I recall my initial ineffectiveness. I had been instructed to secure a temporary ceasefire at a frontline village. I cannot recall its name as we always referred to locations by their grid references. The job was to get the electricity supply reconnected. Houses were burned and destroyed, with villagers living in emergency shelters and children huddling under plastic sheeting in the thick snow. I thought I could fly in and fix it. My approach was urgent and simple, to speak to both parties and agree the resources required, the date and timeline. But after two weeks we had made little progress with resistance coming from both sides. I learned that the textbooks cannot teach you everything. I had barrelled in with solutions before stopping to fully appreciate life from the other side. After some constructive advice, I changed my approach, pausing to create space for people to be heard, to be listened to and for their needs to be acknowledged. Understanding that progress is achieved when you first give people a voice is a fundamental lesson that I still teach about leadership today. Within a matter of days, both parties were willing to oblige and electricity was restored in the village.

Bashkim and I would be invited in to meet the village elders, sitting on small cushions, sipping cups of tea and the KLA's moonshine. The room was always small, usually with one entrance or exit. Women were not normally allowed in, but as the patrol leader, a rare exception was made for me. Every second I spent in those rooms, my heart was racing. The smell of cheap cigarettes still reminds me of the watchful fear I had within me. Amidst the guarded pleasantries there were no guarantees. Yet we gathered so much valuable information by just passing the time with them. We built strong relationships with the locals underpinned by genuine care. It was the key to making others feel safe enough to share. I have no doubt that those connections were also our guardian angel, keeping our patrol away from trouble and giving us an additional pair of eyes. One day, we took a different turn and drove down a track where the KLA had fortified their positions. They fired in our direction, warning shots that skimmed past and forced us to stop. Men ran at us from their trenches and waved at us to turn around. The road was mined. It was the human connection that kept us alive.

As the situation got worse and worse, I found it harder and harder to remain hopeful. There was no ceasefire, no withdrawal of forces and the atrocities were escalating. We could bring in shelter or medical supplies, but that was all we could do. I have no doubt that at times we made the situation worse, and my fear is that our actions cost lives. The Serbian population did not trust us; we were seen to be NATO spies. There were soon reprisals when villagers were seen talking with us. We would often return to a village to find it empty, homes ransacked – my imagination conjured up the horror. People went missing each and every day, families were torn apart with no footprints left to find. The idea of being in Kosovo to monitor a 'ceasefire' became a murderously sick joke.

I struck up a friendship with a Canadian officer called Connor who was also stationed in Peć. Daily patrols were getting laxer and we were given increasing freedom to do what we felt was necessary within our geographical areas. Connor spent his days on rogue patrols and we had arranged to go out on the ground together. A change of scene boosted my morale. The reality was that daily patrols were often monotonous.

A different partner made new conversation – a pleasant change for a while. We had stopped sending in the usual Situation Reports because we knew the Serbian forces were listening in. We understood that we were giving away key information from one side to another each time we shared daily details on the radios. The rogue patrols felt exciting and I wanted more. I felt alive, but I was increasingly vulnerable and playing with fire.

We left Peć early – there had been reports of a Serbian position on the high ground threatening an Albanian village in the valley below. We left the Humvee at the foot of the hill and began to walk up the hillside overlooking the village. The snow had started to melt exposing rocky ground with sparse foliage. Equipped only with a camera, a VHF radio and water bottles, we edged into the dead ground making our way up onto the ridgeline.

Halfway up the hill, something caught my eye. A wire glittered in the sunlight as the breeze moved it. I froze. I followed the wire with my eyes across the ground from left to right in front of me. It came to rest beside a gorse bush anchored to a stake in the soil. There was a wire fixed around it, supporting a white signal cartridge. It was an illume trip wire which would light up the sky, but could do me no damage. But then I saw it – pop, pop, pop – a daisy chain of anti-personnel mines right in front of me and spread out on either side. Time stood still for what seemed like forever, every sinew in my body wanting to scream. My breathing eased as I signalled to Connor. Every feature – each blade of grass, each lump of soil rewound in slow motion. You cannot allow yourself to think of what might happen. You focus on every movement, self-discipline beating down the fear that you cannot acknowledge. With each shuffling step forwards, I boxed it in, contained it, saved it for another time. My focus was the Humvee with my cigarettes on the dashboard, willing me to get down alive.

The journey back down the hillside seemed to take hours. Fear disrupts the natural passing of time. When I reached the Humvee, I lay back, cigarette in hand, lost in my thoughts for a moment as the adrenaline began to subside. Eyes shut, I could hear Connor's breathing beside me. I touched his arm gently, drawing in the perverse excitement and exhaling relief. There is this addictive exhaustion afterwards, knowing that you have got out unscathed. The banter quickly re-started; we sat laughing together, with Connor suggesting an evening of 'a pizza and a pint.' Our laughter soon pushed the events of the day to a more distant memory.

We did head out for pizza and drinks, perhaps in a valiant attempt to restore some semblance of normality to our lives. Life was simple back then, free from righteous judgement on how I chose to spend my nights. We were free from the 'shoulds' and 'should-nots' of what is usually decreed as morally right. A new perspective sharpened its focus and challenged the crumbling tenets of my younger years. Former church paradigms of right and wrong had long since left me. I learned to live in the moment, accepting the ebb and flow, empowered by a new appreciation for the finite fragility of life.

The tour was starting to take its toll. It was cold at -2°C in the day, falling to -10°C at night. The days were long, with none of the usual respite. We were on duty 24/7 and there was no handing over to another patrol. As we drove out of Albanian villages, we would pass the Serbian police and Yugoslav soldiers waiting at the crossroads. They were either drunk or high – or both. The next day we would drive back to the village and find the dead lying in the street and their houses burned to the ground. In the hours in-between, there was no respite in the safety of a military barracks where we could sleep soundly. We were unarmed, living in the community. There was no security. You could never turn off.

In mid-January, we were called to an Albanian village that had been shelled. There were beautiful ornate wooden gates at the entrance to the courtyard. The villagers offered us tea and coffee. It was cold and icy, but there was no snow on the ground. One of the older men led us along a narrow path. He pointed at a house that had a huge hole on a top storey wall. It was oddly round, like a perfect circle. I did not understand exactly what was going on as we were walking in single file, which made it was difficult to follow the translation. The elderly man became increasingly agitated as he led us behind the house. My eyes were glued to the ground, fearful there might be an unexploded shell or a booby trap. He began to point at a white patch of ground. Bashkim was standing next to me, but I did not need an explanation – it was a shallow, open grave. White lime had been scattered on it to try and slow down the rate of decomposition and reduce the smell of decay. The families would move the bodies to a more permanent gravesite when it was safe to travel. The powder covered my feet as I approached and lent over. Red wellington boots pointed skyward, fixed in the ice sheet. Nothing was visible under the water until a man started hitting the thick sheet of ice with a stick. My eyes travelled to the other end of the grave. I could see hair swirling below the surface. The colours were vivid, the red boots, the white lime and the muddy water. I was terrified of seeing her face. Later that night I sat scrubbing my boots, removing every trace of white lime from their surface. I needed to feel clean of it.

All the monitors were soon told to organise their own lodgings in town. Ella and I moved into a rented flat above a baker's shop in the centre, swapping who had the bed and who had the sofa every week. It was unnerving. We were two women alone with none of the normal military back-up. I was constantly checking behind me, scanning the windows and corners. I tried to make myself look strong, walk a little taller and learnt to make my face devoid of expression.

On the surface I was well qualified to perform. I had had some of the best training in the world and had passed the relevant courses. But stripped back, there was nothing left to hide behind – no weapons, no uniform, no rank. It left me feeling naked and exposed. Battling not to show my emotions became the day-to-day norm. There was nothing that we could do. I felt angry.

The Albanian landlord gave us free use of his

landline. It was a reassurance, even though the Serbs were listening in. Yet there was something unnerving about him. We would arrive home and he would appear as if he was expecting us. One evening when I was struggling to light the fire he appeared at the door with fresh kindling, asking if I needed assistance. He didn't live in the building. Certain members of the Albanian community seemed to be left alone and protected by a hidden force. Their property was never shelled or torched. We knew the Serbian police were watching us, but the only way to cope was to put it out of your mind. It was a hall of mirrors. Everyone knew, but no-one said anything. We existed in a bubble, divorced from everything else in our lives.

For a while, the postal service had been non-existent. Then a letter arrived. I was so excited that I waited to open it until the evening when I was on my own at home. I sat on the edge of my bed carefully opening the seal from the side. My first instinct was to laugh out loud, but then I simply felt contempt. The regiment had seen fit to send me a Junior Officers essay paper to complete. There was no 'how are you?', no 'can we do anything?' or 'do you need any help?' I tore up the paper and tossed it in the fire. I cracked open a beer, my contempt festering.

On 15 January, Serbian forces attacked the village of Račak, south of Pristina. The KVM team was refused access and forced to watch the fighting from a nearby hill. When they were finally allowed into Račak, 45 men, a woman and a 12-year-old child lay dead. When William Walker arrived at the scene, he immediately blamed the Serbian police and the Yugoslav Army. He described the massacre as a 'crime very much against humanity'. Belgrade was furious and tried, but failed, to expel him.

Račak changed everything. It led to the convening of a high-level peace conference at a château in Rambouillet outside Paris which, when the Serbs refused to accept the solution suggested by the American, British and French diplomats, in turn led to NATO's 78-day bombing campaign of Serbia and the Serbian retreat from Kosovo.

5

The Ambush

ON 4 FEBRUARY 1999, we prepared for morning patrol. The sky was bright blue and the majestic mountains glistened in the snow. We drove past empty villages and burned-out houses, looted, roofless and graffitied. Then a call came in with a grid reference. There was a report of a possible ambush. I felt a surge of adrenaline and a buzz of excitement as we turned onto the rough, untarmacked road. The snow was so thick it was difficult to follow the track.

When we arrived at the given grid reference nothing seemed unusual. Then we spotted a white Yugo parked before a rickety wooden bridge that led over a stream to the village. We parked a few meters away. I asked Bashkim to stay in the Humvee with the rest of the patrol. I approached the Yugo on foot with Hans, a young German officer. The German soldiers were all well trained and Hans was exceptionally diligent. He was studious and sensitive. I knew he would document the scene carefully.

We walked slowly towards the car, senses acute, eyes scanning for booby traps. Everything was eerily silent and still. Bloody handprints were smeared down the side of the car, sliding down the edge. The boot was ajar, a table sticking out of the back, its legs on either side of the number plate. Glass crunched underfoot. The car windows were shattered. The stench of petrol was choking. To the left of the car, I could see a man's head by the back wheel. He was lying face up, his eyes wide open. His face was grey with a tinge of green bruising, fear fixed in his gaze. The blood on his body was dark. He lay motionless in the snow in bright red, frozen puddles. He had dark brown hair and a stubbly beard and was about 30 years old.

The car door was flung wide open. I could see the exit wound on his right leg. It was twisted back on itself, pointing his foot the wrong way, still hooked into the front of the car. He had been shot as he tried to get out. I wanted to close his deep brown eyes. They made him too real, but I did not have the courage to touch him. I have wished a thousand times that I had done. There was another man, his face down between his legs, stopped in his tracks escaping from the driver's seat. He was small and at first I thought he was a boy.

Then I saw a third man slumped over the gear stick between the two blue front seats. When I put my head in through the smashed window, I saw his leg. The whole of his knee was blown apart. It looked like a joint of meat. I could see the raw bone through the severed ligaments. I felt sick. There was an empty cardboard box on the back seat. The silence and the cold still haunt me.

My head was pounding. Everything had changed and become terrifyingly real. I had never seen death at such a level of intensity. When you get that close it somehow feels personal. I felt a wrenching pain in my throat holding back tears, but I refused to cry. The car had had over 60 bullets fired at it. I became meticulous. Hans was taking notes, even registering that the car's clock had stopped. I can still see the clock.

I tried to put up a cordon, but struggled to fix the mine tape into the frozen ground. There was nothing to wrap it around. I was frightened of booby traps and snipers. Why were we the only people there? It felt like a trap and I was keenly aware that the bright orange Humvee was advertising our presence. I had to take photographs of the men, as evidence. Looking through the lens, zooming in on their faces, it felt like I was encroaching, showing an impertinent lack of respect for the dead.

Then the villagers began to arrive. At first two, then the elders, then more and more people, even children. The cordon started to bulge. There were five of us, unarmed, to keep the peace. The anger was palpable. You could feel it, almost taste it. Still, we were without any additional support. It had been over an hour.

Hans went up to the ridgeline to the right of the bridge where the ambush on the car had most likely taken place. He signalled for me to see what he had found. In the snow, I could see the contours of the gunman's body. The driver, Dan, was still in the Humvee. I radioed back to him. He was a DynCorp man and if anyone could get us out of a tight spot, he was the one. Scattered all around the body were gun cartridges, rounds of 7.62 fired from a Kalashnikov switched to automatic.

Then suddenly, a car screeched to a halt at the back of the crowd and two young men ran towards the scene. They were uncontrollable in their grief. Hysterical. Sobbing. Collapsing to their knees. Every inch of my body wanted to cry with them, but I could not allow myself to feel a thing. There was a crushing tension in my head. There was nothing any of us could do. We just had to stand and watch them. I was unable to offer any comfort, I couldn't find the right words. They then ran back to the car and drove off at high speed.

My attention was suddenly diverted by automatic fire in the near distance. The villagers became agitated. As the anxiety built, Bashkim and I spoke with them, trying to maintain some sense of calm. I was desperate for back-up. All I could do was hold the cordon. I had done everything else expected of me.

Then the Serbian police turned up. They set up their blue armoured personnel carrier on high ground behind with a machine gun pointing down on us as if we were part of the problem. They strode under the cordon and all over the scene. I tried to approach them, but said nothing. What was the point? Relationships had soured to the stage where suspicion drove everything.

Then OSCE personnel from headquarters arrived. There must have been about four or five vehicles. There had been other ambushes that day and we were the next stop. It was as if some of them were sightseeing. People who had been in the office and decided they would come out for a look. Photo snapping for their albums. I stopped them at the Control Point beside my Humvee and took the senior officer forwards to the scene.

As I was briefing him, the same car returned behind the crowd. The two men got out with a group of women. The mother let out an animal-like howl as she saw her boys lying lifeless in the snow. She plunged across the stream in a desperate hurry, distraught, screaming. Her hands were in the air as if imploring some divine being. The two men ran after her to help. She was gasping for air. They were a family utterly devastated and lost in grief. It was terrible to watch. I just wanted to dissolve emotionally. There was nothing that we could do. I felt angry. I could not change a thing. I did not dare to cry, so I held my tears back until my throat ached, until my head was pounding. I turned around to speak to Bashkim, but he was sitting in the snow, his head in his hands. He seemed unable to hear me.

A Serbian policeman came over to the family. Everyone was on edge – you never knew if the concern was genuine, if it was an act, or whether the police already knew everything. There was nothing you could do to pull it apart, to make sense of it. I had a hunch the Serbs had killed the men, but it could just as easily have been the KLA who killed collaborators in the most brutal way. It was impossible to make sense of anything. The senior OSCE officer told me to go over and gather more information from the family. I questioned him as the timing felt insensitive. Then more people turned up. The specialist OSCE Human Rights team, video cameras rolling, captured the scene. The quiet turned into a circus. Everyone trampling over everything. So many agendas. There felt an inconsiderate disrespect for the dead and the family. I went back to the Humvee and sat with Dan, smoking, trying to calm the storm inside of me. Taking refuge in dark humour in an attempt to make light of what was happening.

You get a sixth sense when something is about to happen. It made me hypervigilant. I was always on the lookout for any tell-tale signs. I became addicted to the excitement of what might happen. I started seeing things that were not there. My imagination took over. One day I thought I saw a body lying under a bridge by the side of a road. I said nothing to the rest of the team because we needed to get back, but it kept me awake that night. The next day I went back to search in the shadows, but there was nothing there.

No-one told me what it would be like – the experience of witnessing ethnic cleansing is not easily translated. If anyone had tried to warn me, I would have probably brushed it off. I was young and naïve, but I can still see their faces – not in detail anymore, but their eyes are still present, wide open and searching. The blood is cold in deep puddles on the snow. I can still feel the grief around me, but I can no longer hear their voices. I still feel the fear I felt as I put my head through the window, the crunch of the glass, his face, his knee. And when it comes back, it totally consumes me. My heart races, but my body freezes.

Kosovo was the best of times professionally, and yet Kosovo was the worst of times. I could not accept the deep hatred playing out in front of my eyes. I had dreamt of being a superhero since I was a child on the sports field but, in this nightmare, I could do nothing. We were supposed to be there to make a difference, but we simply watched and listened to the screams and the gunfire. I was gripped by a crushing disillusionment as I betrayed my deepest personal values. I was overwhelmed by guilt. In the chaos there was no clarity, no black or white. Grey was everywhere. Throughout my training I had been groomed to believe that we should be operating according to a higher set of British Army values. But it is difficult to believe that you are one of the 'good guys' when you are forced to stand by and watch war crimes. It was deeply painful to realise that I had bought into a carefully constructed lie. I was a soldier. I was trained to fight. In monitoring there was no agency. All I did was drive out of Peć, talk to people, take photographs and write reports. I went to Kosovo and did virtually nothing to help anyone. I will never come to terms with it. You cannot unsee what you have seen. There is no unseeing.

The next day I went to dinner at one of the French monitors' houses. They killed a chicken in front of me. It was not unusual, but this time it stuck uneasily. There was blood everywhere as the chicken kept running around, flinging its partially severed head up and down the balcony. Later that evening a senior French officer lunged at me. I did all I could to politely reject his advances, but he seemed confused – what was wrong with me? Making my way home, I felt utterly exhausted.

The General in charge of the region complimented me on the way I had handled the scene in his official report, but I felt empty.

Kosovo Verification Mission
Regional Centre 3
Hotel Metropol, Ohrid
Former Yugoslavian Republic of Macedonia

29 Mar 99

END OF MISSION REPORT IN RESPECT OF LIEUTENANT G. LOWTH

POSTS HELD – FUSION OFFICER, PATROL COMMANDER

Lt Lowth joined the Kosovo Verification Mission in December 1998 and after an initial period employed as Personal Assistant to KVM Deputy Head of Mission Operations (and also Commander BRITCON), she was subsequently posted to Regional Centre 3 in Pec, Western Kosovo. Her performance throughout the mission was outstanding. Upon arrival in Pec she was initially employed as a fusion (intelligence) officer and contributed significantly to the effectiveness of RC 3 across its entire AOR. She worked tirelessly to ensure that information gleaned from patrol personnel. Additionally she gave strong support to the non-native English speakers amongst her colleagues and was proactive and forward looking in her approach to her multitude of tasks. Lowth's work ethic was extremely strong and she regularly went on patrol to both enhance her knowledge of the AOR and to help alleviate the burden on patrol members. Throughout her time as a fusion officer, Lowth demonstrated an excellent grasp of all operational aspects of her employment.

Later in January 99, Lowth was transferred to a new role and became a patrol commander in the Decane Co-ordination Centre, with responsibility for the execution of the mission plan within her own AOR. Patrol leadership is always demanding, often frustrating and occasionally dangerous; however, good patrol leadership is second nature to Lowth and she quickly applied her dynamic, positive and uncompromising attitude to this new task. Lowth's performance as a patrol commander was exceptional. A thorough planner and reporter, she contributed valuable new information to the mission and gave valued and meaningful interpretations of events and incidents. Calm in any situation, Lowth often found her team in dangerous and difficult environments and extracted them in good order every time. This capacity for clarity of thought and effectiveness under pressure was demonstrated on many occasions the most notable of which was her commendable handling of the scene of an ambush where her quickness of thought, clarity of orders and firm handling of the Serb authorities brought high praise from many experienced crime scene experts.. Lowth's activities were not limited to her verification duties and her efforts in the humanitarian arena were considerable; she became known in the local villages as Djamelia, "the bringer of good and hope". Lowth was always aware of the humanitarian situation in the Albanian villages within her AOR, many of which were destroyed and suffering from a lack of co-ordination between humanitarian agencies. Her quick intervention, personal interest and follow-up immediately remedied these problems. By the time of the mission evacuation, Lowth had succeeded in reducing the level of fear amongst returning villagers and was actively involved in day-to-day village activities; successful and delicate negotiations with nearby Serb police checkpoints were an integral part of this process.

Throughout her time with the KVM, Lowth has made significant personnel contribution to the Effort and is, by any standard, an officer who demonstrates tremendous potential for future command responsibility. It has been a pleasure working with this fine ambassador of her country whose capacity for innovative thought and independent action single her out as a special individual.

Edward Szwargrzyk
(Major General, Polish Army)
Regional Centre 3 Commander

6

Eyes Wide Open

THE AMBUSH AND the injustice of it all simply emboldened me. I began finding excuses to patrol in ever more dangerous places, like a child placing their hand in the fire.

I had grown too close to the Albanian community. I had been drawn into what was happening and allowed myself to feel it, to let it in. Patrolling became a visceral, animal-like existence. I wanted to go after them, to take revenge. I needed to hold to account the people that had done such indescribable things. It became a futile, dangerous game of cat and mouse. We would chase down the evidence, they would watch us and wait until darkness to move again. It was the human dimension that got to me, the inescapable reality that these were human beings. The worst part was that I was convinced that the people who had carried out these acts would get away with it.

Not that it was easy to deal with Kosovo Liberation Army commanders. The KLA had no real military structure. They were dressed in army fatigues one minute and then in civilian clothes the next. First you had to find the commanders. Everything was covered in a veil of secrecy and even when you were introduced to someone who you were told was the commander, it was difficult to judge if they really were who they said they were, and at times both parties were as tricky as each other.

One afternoon, deep inside KLA territory, we stopped at a shop to chat with the locals. We were talking with the family who ran the store when suddenly a KLA commander forced his way past me, shouting and pointing his weapon at the shopkeeper. He demanded that we left immediately and went back to base. We were escorting a Non-governmental Organisation (NGO) with much needed makeshift tents to house people whose homes had been destroyed by Serbian shells. I went back to the Humvee and sat there silently, the anger raging inside me. Then something clicked. I stormed back in to confront him. The commander was an enormous man and he waved his Kalashnikov rifle at me as if it was an extension of his hand. At that moment, the shopkeeper's toddler son slipped out from behind the counter and took hold of my hand. I looked down at his face. His eyes were full of the horrors he had witnessed and yet his presence cut through the hostility. The KLA commander quietened and allowed us to continue with the NGO. Bashkim was furious I had taken such a risk. The others said nothing.

One evening after work, two American DynCorp monitors I had become friendly with, Max and Rob, came over to go out for something to eat. They were based in the Peć HQ but exactly what they got up to I never found out, as I knew it was best not to ask too many questions.

I was feeling tired and uptight. I had just picked up eight letters from home that had all arrived on the same day. Up until then there had been two months of silence. I wanted to speak to my family. It had been such a long time since I had heard their voices. Max and Rob lent me their vehicle. I dropped them at the café and went back to headquarters to try and make the call. Few had mobile phones then, but Doc had a satellite phone which meant I could have a private conversation. I tried for hours to get through. Eventually, I managed to say hello to my parents only to be immediately cut off. Frustrated, I drove back at high speed to the café.

I parked a short distance away. It was dark. There were no streetlamps. It was raining, the road was wet. Within moments I realised I was being followed. A mix of Serbian and broken English, their voices were aggressive and raised, trying to get my attention. I turned around. Three young men were walking in the middle of the road, drunk and gesticulating. One was clearly the leader. He was taller and more domineering than the rest. I turned back quickly towards the car. I walked fast and determinedly suppressing the urge to run, panic building in my chest. I started the engine, terrified that they would force their way into the car with me before I had time to lock the doors and drive away. I pulled up directly in front of the café.

Relieved, I sat down next to Max and Rob, my back to the entrance. I warned them there was trouble outside. There were mirrors on the back wall where I could see the street behind me. Another group of OSCE staff were sitting at another table.

The three men walked in. They closed the door and strode over to our table. The tall one came up behind me and placed his hands on my shoulders. He was wearing a black leather jacket with an OSCE pass around his neck. I sat still, eyes fixed on the mirror and at Max and Rob, hoping that they would stay calm and let it be. Rob asked the man to show his identification. He started laughing, his hands pushing down on me. He leant into my neck, his left hand moving down along my arm. He felt unshaven and smelt of alcohol and cigarettes. Everyone in the café was watching but no-one moved. It was the last thing I wanted them to do. I was terrified things would escalate out of control.

From the other table, Jack, a Canadian who worked in the HQ operations room, got up and tried to reason with the man. I felt alert but drained, just wanting it to end. As Jack stood up, the tall Serb took his hands off my shoulders. His hand moved to his right-hand pocket. He pulled out a pistol grip – not the whole piece, but just enough to make Jack sit down. I felt trapped, rigid in my seat. There was no escape. The three men were standing between our table and the door. The only way out was through the back. One of the OSCE men from the other table moved back towards the lavatory carrying his hand-held radio. Meanwhile, everything the Serb said continued to be directed at me. He kept moving my hair to expose my neck. I could feel the warmth of his breath as he leant down towards me. I looked straight ahead, my heart racing, staring at the mirror. Each time he moved closer, I smelled the alcohol and cigarettes. Then I turned to him, still seated, and asked him to leave. He just started laughing, all three of the men simply laughed at me. It was demeaning. There was nothing I could do. There was nothing anyone could do. If he wanted it, he would take what he needed.

A Serbian policeman in uniform sat in the corner, watching the whole scene. Jack stood up again. His female interpreter was sitting beside him. The tall Serb went up to her and forced her arm behind her back. He told her he was going to break it. With their focus on the other table, we had space to get out. I stood up, terrified to turn my back on him. Petrified he would follow. But they stayed. Nothing happened. OSCE vehicles arrived to escort the others home. We drove away.

Going to sleep that night I felt detached, numb and emotionally drained. All I had wanted was to speak to someone from home, to regain some small window of normality. I lay there unable to think. Ella was away on leave, so I was alone in the apartment. That night, my doorbell kept ringing. Alone and unarmed in the centre of Peć with a handheld radio that rarely had any signal, I could not sleep.

The next day, Rob filed a harassment case against the tall Serb from the mission staff. He had been hired to drive an ambulance, but when they looked into him more closely they discovered that he was actually a member of the Serbian police. I was called in and told not to be alone, to make sure I was always with somebody. With Ella away that was impossible. People were sympathetic, but there was simply no back-up. I had to look after myself.

In the weeks that followed the doorbell rang during the night, but I never moved towards the door. I never looked outside. Sporadic bouts of automatic fire would dance right outside my window. I was certain that they were watching me. I would sleep in a half sleep each night, dozing but still awake, listening to the sound of footsteps or gunfire approaching. The situation was getting increasingly dangerous and we had become a target. We were given orders to be back in Peć before nightfall.

Max would often come back home with me and check the apartment, but no-one moved in permanently over those weeks. The strange thing was that I never asked Max much about himself – secrecy clouded everything. There was no long-term planning or trivia to distract from the intensity of the moment. Being with Max, I could relax, let go for precious moments, loosing myself against his body, feeling safe temporarily. The touch of another human brought a relief like no other. It was as if nothing else mattered.

But we were never truly alone. When the intrusion started, it was timed to perfection. The explosion of bullets below my window made us hit the floor and take cover on our hands and knees. Scrambling for our clothes, we huddled together against the wall. We listened to Serbian soldiers laughing. It was humiliating. They were watching every intimate moment. There was nowhere to escape. No privacy.

The Serbian police were responsible for our security. They knew everything. I was constantly watching my back on high alert. I could not relax for a second. There was no safe place to be. Walking into the apartment each night I checked everywhere, behind the doors, in cupboards, under everything. Checking that my possessions were where I had left them, where they should have been.

The real problem was that what happened in the café had brought back uncomfortable memories of incidents that had happened in the barracks back home. They were a dangerous addition to the mix. I started to play with them, to play them out and try to change the endings. I tried to harness the anger to keep me safe. I became more aggressive. It helped me feel stronger, stifling my fear, but it confused my thinking and made it harder to make sense of things.

After the evening in the café, things changed. I started looking for trouble. I would do things that I knew were unsafe. Drink in a bar and then walk home alone. Out patrolling, I stopped taking 'no' for an answer. I had had enough of sitting back and trying to accommodate. I pushed the boundaries. My anger grew and I began to step over the line, to push harder or even provoke. I almost wanted something to happen. I was seeking an opportunity to take back control and put the record straight.

When we patrolled beyond the frontline, I turned our radios off. I knew that the Serbian forces were listening in and I wanted to deny them more information. I set out on patrols looking for action. It was addictive. I was hoping for something to happen, choosing locations where the threat was at its highest. Each day, adrenaline seeking.

Although the diplomatic moves to resolve the conflict had already begun in February at the château in Rambouillet, not far from Paris, the talks had broken down less than a month later. I was at a Serbian checkpoint on the frontline while I waited to hear the result of the negotiations on the radio. I knew things were going badly wrong in Rambouillet, but we sat with the soldiers, smiling and drinking tea, calming every instinct to get out immediately.

Just before NATO launched its first ever war, Ella and I were collected from Peć early one morning and taken back to Pristina. I was getting ready to go home on some leave when two monitors arrived to escort us. One was British Special Forces and the other an Italian operative. We stayed with them overnight and then they escorted me to the airport to fly back to the UK. They watched me go through the gate and even called my father to check that I was back in the UK. I can only assume that they were concerned for my safety. One of the female interpreters had been shot in the back of the head. I continually heard rumours our names were on a Serbian hit list, but nobody ever explained any more. All I knew was that I was home on leave for two weeks.

7

The Unravelling

AT FIRST MY parents were relieved to have me home. My father had cut out and saved every article about the conflict that had appeared in *The Times* while I was in Kosovo. I still have them in a box. He was the same dad who used to cheer me on at the touchline and discuss the game on the way home. But I had been playing a game he did not really understand, and I was not the same person.

At first, I felt this irresistible urge to talk for hours to anyone who would listen. It would all come tumbling out. I met an old friend from church, my former youth leader, for a drink. I took my photograph album with me and showed her picture after picture. The blood and gore were totally out of place in a cosy home counties pub. She sat there in silence. People had no idea what to say and soon stopped asking. There was no-one to share it with, so I kept everything bottled up inside me. It distanced me from my family and friends.

While I was home the KVM mission was evacuated to Macedonia. NATO leaders thought that it would take a couple of days of airstrikes to bring the Serbs back to the negotiating table and that the mission would soon be redeployed in a peacekeeping role. What followed was a 78-day campaign of high-tech air strikes against Serbia.

My KVM colleagues spent three weeks debriefing and decompressing together in Macedonia. I was alone in England and totally isolated. That isolation would have devastating consequences.

The situation deteriorated rapidly after we left. Sitting at home, I was even more powerless than ever. I sat glued to the TV, reading everything in the newspapers, every update to find out what had happened. I spent hours scouring OSCE reports for information. I went back to my photographs and interviews repeatedly. I was obsessed with Kosovo and what was happening, as if my memory needed to be constantly refreshed.

Then on 1 April 1999, Serbian police and paramilitaries, some wearing bandanas, some dark glasses, entered the village of Ljubenić on the road between Deçan and Peć. I knew it well. Albanian men from Peć and the surrounding areas were already being marched along the highway towards Ljubenić. Among them were many of the locals who had worked for us. As soon as I heard this, I was convinced that Bashkim was among them. The villagers tried to flee into the forests, but found themselves surrounded. They were ordered to gather in the centre of the village near the mosque. Once the men from Peć arrived, the women and children were separated from them. The men were then lined up against a wall. They were ordered to lie down, and then shot. I was frightened that Bashkim had been killed. That it was my fault. That I had left him behind whilst we had evacuated. That I had failed in my duty of care. I became obsessed with finding out what had happened to him, but there was no way to trace him. I didn't even know his surname.

I was left with a terrible sense of guilt eating away at me.

I began to struggle to do the simplest things. My mother asked me to pick up some shopping in the local Sainsbury's. She had written biscuits on the list. I dithered in front of an array of different packets totally unable to choose. I was exhausted, but could not sleep. There is a photograph of me sitting on my parents' sofa. The eyes give me away. I am vacant and unfocused, looking beyond the camera lens towards a different sense of reality.

Before I went to Kosovo, I had a deep Christian faith. My family did not go to church in those days apart from at Christmas and Easter, but as a teenager at an all-girls school I had joined the local Christian youth group in the hope of meeting some boys. I made close friends, and my faith grew out of that. The congregation had even prayed for me while I was in Kosovo.

When I came home, I went to the local church and sat in the back pew. I stared at the three angels in the stained-glass windows and the tears began to well up in my eyes. When I went to services the music made me cry. I would try everything to hold onto my emotions, biting my lip or pinching my skin, to not let others see. People would come up to me and hug me. I hated it, so I stopped going. I turned off my faith. I could not reconcile faith in God with such suffering. I could not face the emotional task of thinking through it, so I simply disconnected. I hid from the difficult questions. I turned off the music too. Until Kosovo, music had been a key part of my life, but I could no longer bring myself to sing or play the piano. It brought out too many emotions that I was not prepared to deal with.

When my two-week break was up, the Regiment called me and told me to report back to Abingdon. All the other British soldiers on the mission were given post-deployment leave when they returned to Britain, but I was not. It never entered their head that I was entitled to it, and to be honest I did not push for it either. I wanted to be sent back to Kosovo. There was no follow up, no checking in to see if I was alright, no psychological debrief. Absolutely nothing. One minute I was in Kosovo and the next I was driving to work in Oxfordshire.

I was the only soldier from my regiment who had been deployed to Kosovo as part of the KVM. The rest of the regiment assumed that the deployment had been similar to their experiences in Bosnia, which at the time was fairly routine and uneventful. They had been part of the NATO-led multinational peacekeeping forces who were sent after the war had ended. Most of my peers had only seen the aftermath of war. They had no idea what it was like to be deployed in civilian clothes with no back-up infrastructure in the middle of the blood and the maiming. It was extremely unusual to have been deployed in a conflict zone in such a way, but the Army had never really understood what they were sending us to do and seemed oblivious to its consequences.

I expected to go back to Kosovo as a liaison officer

with NATO once the bombing stopped, but the call never came, even though the rest of the regiment were preparing to deploy. I was left completely in the dark and given no explanation, not even when a stony-faced woman in civilian clothing arrived to take all my maps, my notes and photographs. I had copied everything but the maps, so did not put up a protest. At the time I had no idea that there had been a death threat made towards me. The first time I heard anything about it was at a Mess function at Deepcut in 2021. A drunken officer, who had been working at Joint Headquarters at the time, started to talk. I pressed him for more information, but he clammed up suddenly. That was the last that I heard from anyone about the KVM ever again.

To have been sent back to Kosovo would have been better for me. I was fine when I was out there. I managed to keep the wheels turning alongside people who shared similar experiences. In Britain, the qualities that served me well in Kosovo defeated me. The problems started when I returned to a world that moved at a different pace.

The regiment had not expected me back so early, so there was no job waiting for me and not a single troop to lead. Random meaningless assignments came my way. I was sent to itemise the silverware in the Officers' Mess. Folder in hand and a silver spoon in the other, a rising sense of contempt grew within me. I began to ignore the boundaries and the fierce work ethic that had guided my former life. Alone and isolated, I was unmoored with nothing and no-one to anchor my emotions. I started to question my career and my relationships. I was ordered to do the 'March & Shoot', a key test of physical endurance and weapon skill. Once I would have loved it, but now I held my rifle with ill-disciplined scorn and derision. I felt as if I was drowning in a pointless, meaningless monotony. The world that had meant so much to me was just not credible anymore.

One weekend, my parents invited me for a family Sunday lunch. As the joint of lamb was placed in front on me, all I could see was the man's knee in the front of the car, blown apart, blood seeping down the sides of his leg. I began to panic. I felt a retching sensation and wanted to run from the room, but I simply froze. To deal with the images running in my mind, I began to remove myself from reality, to disengage. I was physically present in the dining room, but if you had asked me a question you would have been talking to a ghost.

I needed to slow down, but the quiet frightened me. I had learned to survive by racing forwards, running like crazy to escape. I was promoted and, in April 1999, I took a new job at Dalton Barracks as an Administrative Officer in the HQ of 6 Transport Squadron. Not long after, I was awarded the Carmen Sword as the best-ranked young officer in the Royal Logistic Corps. I was the first woman to win the award. I was over the moon. I had proved myself. At the ceremony I was presented with a beautifully etched sword by the Princess Royal. I loved the recognition that awards brought. I always had. I needed them.

No-one seemed to notice that I was doped up to the eyeballs – vodka, Valium, sleeping pills and anti-depressants – anything to escape and numb the pain.

The flashbacks started as soon as I went to sleep. In my dreams I could see the red wellington boots sticking up out of the frozen, muddy water, the limestone and the woman's hair swirling as the ice broke. Panic gripped me as she began to raise her head. I woke in terror, terrified I would see her face. I started drinking. I drank to forget. I would avoid going to sleep until I was so lubricated that I no longer had to try. Then two hours later I was awake. I would spend the rest of the night on the floor, knees to chest, gently rocking, trying to numb my mind. I resorted to sleeping pills, but the mornings became unbearable. The pills were a deadly mix with the alcohol. I woke with a splitting headache and was groggy and lethargic for hours. On bad nights I simply lay awake. My fitness scores tumbled. I struggled to concentrate. I was the first in the bar, earlier and earlier, every night.

The nightmares haunted more than the memories. The dreams were more vivid, more real. In my dreams I was standing beside the white Yugo or staring at the ice in the death pit night after night. Silent fragments of unwanted recollection. A sudden flash, the kind that confuses past and present. The smell, the blood, the faces, the colours.

I hid myself away from the world. At night I began to camp out in the woods. Through the long nights I would sit for hours, tucked up on the floor, staring at the canvas. I had no idea what was happening to me. I was too frightened to tell anyone in case they thought less of me. My failures became an ever-present chant running through my head. I was full of regret and remorse, but frightened that I could not remember things clearly. I was confused by the images that ran through my dreams. Were they real or was I imagining them. Maybe if I was back there and not here, I would have a chance to fix what felt like my mistakes. Maybe if I knew what had happened to Bashkim, it would put an end to my nightmares. I could not even walk down the local high street without mistaking a manhole cover for a mine. The demons came in many guises – guilt, shame and rage. Everything at home seemed inconsequential and irrelevant. It made me angry and resentful of everyone around me.

The Canadian officers from Peć got in contact as they passed through London. Ella came to visit for the day, but I kept everything to myself. I held her at arm's length. I did not want to seem weak. I went for a drink in London with a couple of the men. Among them was Connor with whom I had found myself trapped on the hillside, surrounded by a daisy chain of mines. We had a few drinks at the pub and I went back to their apartment. They were working as liaison officers with NATO. The conversation was non-stop and emotional. Their sympathies lay more than ever with the Albanians. Hans, the German officer who had been at the site of the white car with me, wrote me a letter. I decided not to reply. I regret it. Maybe he was brave enough to reach out to someone, but I was not. I cut myself off from all of them in a fruitless attempt to play the tough guy.

Behind the façade, I was running on empty and engaging in every self-destructive behaviour that you could name. One night I was out drinking with other officers and we ended up at a party in a house on the married quarters. A married officer grabbed my hand and led me out, pulling me across the back gardens to his house to get another drink. Jumping over the picket fences, I just went with it. It was not clear at first that we were the only ones leaving. Once inside, he led me straight upstairs. I was unsteady, the walls were shifting. There was a small room next to his. It had an unoccupied cot inside the door. He started to unbutton my trousers and undress me. Struggling to stand, I did nothing to stop him. Drifting in and out of consciousness, I let it happen. I lay still, fixing my eyes beyond him and onto the ceiling. My body betrayed me. I pulled on my trousers, stuffing my underwear into my pocket and left saying nothing. Walking home dishevelled in the dark, I started to cry. Not the usual tears, but deep shame and confusion retching from me.

The next day he appeared in my room and asked me to get the morning after pill. Somehow he seemed more sensitive, more caring. All he wanted was that there were no repercussions. I went to the medical centre that morning and broke down with the nurse who was caring for me. She never probed about the circumstance. Our conversation was about taking responsibility for contraception rather than consent. I walked away with the morning after pill, some leaflets and a number for the Army Welfare Service.

The atmosphere in barracks was as toxic as ever. One morning, I gave my passport to the clerk for administration. When I came back from lunch, an image of my face superimposed on a naked porn star's body was stuck up all over the building. The men thought it was hilarious. At formal dinners, pranks were the main entertainment and I was fair game. One night when I was personally hosting a senior officer's wife, as the place mats were cleared, a hard-core pornographic image was revealed underneath, laminated to the table. I apologised to her, but she pretended not to have noticed. Mortified, I had to sit there, with it looking back at me, enduring the toasts. If you complained it just made you a greater target.

One day I took a call from the Regimental Headquarters. When I put the phone down, I had no idea what I had just been told to do. I was struggling to concentrate or retain detailed information. I broke down just as a colleague walked into my office. He suggested that I went to the medical centre. The doctor was unable to recall my name and continually called me Genna. His report said that since returning from Kosovo I had suffered from insomnia and flashbacks and that he thought I had mild PTSD and depression. In the notes he wrote 'PTDS', spelling the diagnosis incorrectly. It was a give-away for how little he understood. He gave me ten days sick leave and referred me to the Department of Community Psychiatry at Aldershot.

The Community Psychiatric Nurse summed up her first impression of me: 'A 26-year-old officer who appears to be experiencing post traumatic reaction in response to her observer role in Kosovo.' I was put on a course of Re-exposure Therapy, a technique that is now considered extremely damaging. She asked me to describe the ambush and bring in the photographs I had taken. She recorded what I told her on a cassette and told me to listen to it every night. I was prescribed anti-depressants. The re-exposure set off a chain reaction, merging the real with the imagined, the past with the present. The session would stop punctually and abruptly. I would leave in an increasingly dangerous state of mind.

I began seeing things. For a split second a discarded pair of shoes or shadow in a doorway took me back to Kosovo. Albanians leave their shoes by the doors of their houses. Often, we returned to villages where we had drunk coffee with the locals the day before to find the doors to the houses were wide open, belongings strewn across the floor, drawers open, beds stripped and a row of empty shoes lined up neatly by the door. The children's shoes were the saddest. We would search the outbuildings, terrified we would find the family murdered in the barn. I never did find them, but in my mind's eye I could imagine the worst. It is not always what you see that haunts you. The sense of failure and that I had been powerless to protect them was always lurking around the corner waiting to catch me. I was constantly on edge and primed.

Then I took an overdose. I wouldn't describe it as a deliberate attempt to die; I just couldn't cope with living anymore. I was sent home to my parents for two weeks' sick leave. My parents had made my room as nice as they could and my mother cooked for me. Their love was quiet and watchful. They did not probe or ask questions. They had instructions to give me my medication, but were given no other advice on how to care for me. I was ashamed and uncommunicative, and they allowed me to be. I was no longer the girl they knew, and I was not an easy person to be around. They had always been involved in my life before the Army, but the Army divorce you from your family and replace them. My parents resented the way the Army had taken over my life. The Army had driven a wedge between us just when I needed them most.

Then once back in barracks, I took too many tablets for a second time. I spent the night in the hospital in Aldershot, where I overheard the psychiatrist discussing my symptoms in the corridor with the nurse. He said that he couldn't understand why I was behaving in this way as I had so much going for me. His tone felt dismissive and patronising. I listened whilst he went on to share details of another patient who was lying in the room next to me.

When I returned to barracks in Abingdon, my troop Sergeant warned me that people were gossiping about me in the Sergeants' Mess. I had no-one to talk to. When pastoral support should have been there to catch me as I fell, it was lacking. It was well known that doctors and chaplains breached confidentiality under the guise of maintaining 'fighting effectiveness'. True to form, my medical details had been shared with the chain of command and then further. The gossip shattered my credibility and overwhelmed what little dignity I had managed to preserve. There was no confidentiality and nowhere to hide. The shame and the desperation ate away at my self-worth and destroyed what was left of my identity. I had invested everything in the Army, but they judged me to be a failure in the most public way they could.

Then David Morgan walked back into my life.

8

The Betrayal

I HAD MET David in 1997 when we were both young lieutenants at Dalton Barracks, long before I went to Kosovo. He was on a familiarisation visit to the Officers' Mess and I was asked to show him around. I was impressed by his black MR2 sports car and green Kawaski Ninja Motorbike, but there was more to David than that. He had far less of his alpha male ego on display than the other men. He was humble, cautious, quietly confident and considered. We became close friends, but were both in relationships with other people.

In October 1999, just as my life was in free fall, we went for drinks with a group of officers in town. We left the pub together and grabbed a taxi. His room was directly below mine in the Officers' Mess, but he had an espresso machine. We made coffee and sat together, chatting into the early hours. When I stood up to leave, there was a moment of uncertainty as we looked at each other awkwardly. There was this unspoken chemistry beyond our friendship that we were cautious to entertain. After what seemed like forever, I asked him if he was going to kiss me. He said he thought I was out of his league. We laughed and moved closer.

We did everything we could to keep the relationship quiet. I felt safe and secure with him. I knew he genuinely cared about me. He asked me to see the ABBA tribute band, Bjorn Again, in Oxford. We were up on our feet singing and dancing. We shared a kiss and when I turned around, I saw some of the other officers from the base. We were rumbled.

He knew that I was struggling as we had written to each other while I was in Kosovo, but he was not aware of how bad the situation was getting. David had been deployed to Kosovo with NATO immediately on my return, leaving six months for my health to deteriorate quietly.

When I was with him, I felt stable and secure. He was fit and strong, but I never felt threatened by him. When I first told him I loved him it just slipped out. We were walking back from lunch in the Officers' Mess down a long side corridor. He leant to kiss me as he went back to his office. As he did, I said, 'I love you.' I shocked myself and pulled back embarrassed. He did the decent thing and pretended that he had not heard. It was a turning point and we stopped trying to hide the strength of our feelings.

I was aggressive and had violent rages. I tried to control it by running, loud music playing in my head-phones. During Christmas leave, I snapped. My mother had made a batch of mince pies. It had taken hours. I had watched her do it. When they were all in the oven she went upstairs and asked me to take them out when they were ready. I forgot and when she came down, they were burnt. She was rightly angry with me, but I overreacted. I flung the mince pies across the kitchen yelling that last Christmas I was picking up bodies and could not care less about her mince pies. She withdrew up to her bedroom. There was a period of quiet and I went into her room to apologise. Something triggered me and in seconds I had her up against her bedroom cupboards. They were white, built in around the bed. I had her by her neck. I was shouting right into her face. Then I came to my senses and recoiled mortified and ashamed. After that I think she was frightened of me and pulled away. I felt I was to blame. My family were bewildered and confused. They struggled, and still do, to understand what had happened to me. I have never been able to share the details with them. When I tried to tell my mother she made herself busy as if she did not want to hear what I had to say. She became increasingly angry and frustrated that the Army were not reaching out to take care of me as she thought they should.

It was all about to get much worse, but first something wonderful happened. I went on holiday with David to the Canary Islands. It was our first time on holiday together. We had a small apartment next to the sand dunes, running together every morning and lying in the sunshine for much of the day. Sitting on the beach watching the Millennium fireworks, we held each other looking up at the sky. I realised that he was the man I wanted to marry and within a few months we were engaged.

In the new year, my parents were called in for a meeting with the Community Psychiatric Nurse. I was told to sit outside the room and wait whilst they discussed me. Sitting in that waiting room, I felt ashamed to my core and completely disempowered. I was considered at risk of suicide and so they suggested two options. The first was to admit me to the Army psychiatric hospital in Catterick, but this would end my career. The second was to send me home on two weeks' leave, but only if my parents would sign responsibility for me. During the meeting she made it clear that the Army was not responsible for my illness. My notes read that I 'was not personally traumatised (in Kosovo), but found it very difficult to cope with the responsibilities' that I encountered. PTSD was never mentioned nor was the Re-Exposure Therapy that I had been subjected to. The psychiatrist wrote that I was experiencing a moderate depressive mood disorder unrelated to my army experience, more likely as a result of genetic predisposition.

My parents were angry and concerned that I had colluded in the diagnosis. At the time I was so sucked into army life that I was unaware of the narrative that the Army were now spinning. I never even considered seeking a second medical opinion. We walked out of the barracks together, although I was left to follow a few steps behind. On the drive home, I sat in the back seat of the car and nothing was said. The experience had left a simmering anger between us.

Nevertheless, I still believed in the Army. I wanted to succeed and rise in the ranks. In April I took a new job at the now notorious Deepcut Barracks in Surrey, where between 1995 and 2002 four young recruits died of gunshot wounds. I had still not really understood the misogyny that surrounded me. Pay was equal, but I was about to learn that opportunities were not. No sooner had I unpacked my kit, than I was called into the Regimental Headquarters. The Colonel welcomed me and smiled, but said that I would not be given the promised officer recruitment role I had been assigned. He did not want a girl to be the face of the Corps. I remember his words precisely: I was 'the best person for the job, but not the right person'. This was the face of the Royal Logistic Corps, the largest Corps of the British Army. It made no sense. By awarding me the Carmen Sword they had ranked me as the best young officer. Now, I felt cast aside because of my gender. He said that I could have the soldier recruitment role instead as it was less high profile.

In mid-May it was time for my psychiatric review. The psychiatrist wrote in his notes that I looked stressed and unhappy. 'Her facial colour was rather high. Remains angry. Put down to alcohol use.' I was diagnosed with 'Affective Disorder with Associated Harmful use of Alcohol'. I was drinking about 40 units a week, but this was far from unusual in military circles. Regardless, the psychiatrist referred me to the Alcohol Treatment Unit. He downgraded me to non-deployable status and said, 'it must be considered permanent.' I had been awarded a Regular Commission, which meant a guaranteed job until retirement, but this blocked any future promotion. By stating that my diagnosis was not attributable to military service, I was not even eligible for medical discharge or compensation. It was the ultimate betrayal. They wanted to move the problem on. I have since discovered that I was not the only person to be treated in such a manner. It was a discernible trend. The Army was shirking its responsibilities on a far wider scale than I knew at the time.

Nevertheless, I still felt a sense of deep loyalty and tried to get on with the job. In April 2001, David and I were married. I wore white and David wore his 'blues'. It was a traditional wedding in our local church. Not long after, I convinced my Commanding Officer to send me back to Kosovo to perform a week-long administrative role that was not considered as deployment. I persuaded him that we needed fresh images of our soldiers working on the ground to help raise the profile of the new marketing campaign.

David was supportive. He thought it was a good idea to get some closure. No-one questioned it. As far as they were concerned, I was just going out there for a few weeks to work with some photographers. I did not tell the Community Psychiatric Nurse. When I came back she raised an eyebrow, but that was that.

There was no closure. Kosovo was completely different, almost unrecognisable. The dynamic had turned on its head now the Albanian community were in power. Red flags with black Albanian eagles on them flew all over the city. I began to see just how complicated the political history of the region was and how little I knew about it. I was different too. This time I was in uniform, ranked and armed. I was based in an organised military camp with rules and restrictions and was not allowed to go back to Peć.

One thing travelled with me – the sexual harassment. The civilian photographer we had hired looked on astounded while a male officer in the front of the Land Rover kept creating sexual scenarios for me to respond to. I was the entertainment.

It escalated in the evenings when I was in the Officers' Mess, where he became more physical. There was nowhere to escape to other than locking myself in my bedroom. I dashed in and out of the shared bathroom as fast as I could. Even though I was now a married woman, it did not stop. Every morning I felt degraded, humiliated, as he laughed with his men, taking live verbal odds on what he might have done to me that night. It was persistent and seemingly endless. It continued to grind me down just at the moment I was in need of support from my brothers in arms.

Not long after I got back from Kosovo, I found out I was pregnant. I had always wanted to have children and it felt wonderful. I found out while we were on holiday on the Isle of Wight. Shortly afterwards David was deployed to Bosnia as the Senior Ammunition Technical Officer. It was an important job and he needed to stay focused.

When I got back to Deepcut, I went to the medical centre for an official test. I asked for the results to remain confidential. I had a desk job and wanted to be in control my own life. But in the time it took for me to walk back from the medical centre to my office, my Commanding Officer had been informed. He called me in to see him. He seemed surprised and asked if it was planned or a mistake. It may be a shocking thing to say today, but until 1993 being pregnant had been a sackable offence.

People's attitude to me changed immediately. I could no longer wear my uniform, so I wore ordinary clothes. It made me stand out, made me an outsider. I was the first of my young female officer group to get pregnant. I was no longer invited out by my peers. I stopped smoking and drinking immediately, but it was the cold shoulder that hurt. Then I was passed over for job opportunities, as I had needed to get a sick chit for light duties. There was an overall sense that I was malingering – the dreaded biff. Soon my health began deteriorating. I was referred back to Aldershot for a review. The Deepcut Medical Officer concluded 'She is presently in a deeply despondent state. I have grave doubts about her future ability to return to work.' David was called home on compassionate leave and swiftly ejected from his Regiment, 11EOD, the Army's specialist unit responsible for improvised explosive device and conventional munitions disposal. His Commanding Officer was fearful that he might be distracted and did not want him working with explosives. Devastated, he was forced to take a dead-end desk job. He had worked and trained so hard for the specialist role, but he took the job to support me and our new family.

We would lie together watching the baby do somersaults inside my tummy, laughing out loud. But it was also a time of enormous uncertainty. I was extremely lonely. My head was all over the place and my career was in danger. I never wanted to leave the Army at this vulnerable time. Civilian life scared me. I wanted support to stay inside, but there was no duty of care. The brotherhood scattered as if I had a contagious disease. There was no military family. I had been sold a myth and spun a web of lies. I lost faith in 'Queen and Country'; the sacred promise that the Army would take care of its own was a vacuous lie. The commissioning scroll that sat on my wall, neatly framed with the Queen's signature at the bottom, mocked me. It violated everything that I had been taught to believe. There was Kosovo, but what came after, the way the Army treated me, was far more significant and far more traumatising. The psychiatrist wrote, 'Gemma is an anxious, emotionally insecure, introverted personality.' He continued, 'The mental well-being of people like Gemma can be poised on a knife edge between health and despair.' They undermined every piece of me bit by bit until I started to question everything I had known.

It is easy for the instructors in training to tell you to 'do the right thing'. They do not tell you that it may come at the expense of your family, your future and your sanity. What they do not say is that if that right thing challenges the system, you need to be willing to pay the price. They did not want to acknowledge that they had been at fault. They wanted me to stay quiet and go away.

I was pulled in all directions and had no idea what I wanted anymore. I could not stop crying. I agonised about ending my career. I was so proud to be an Army officer and I admired the institution. Loyalty to the

Army is important and it carries a tremendous amount of pressure. I liked so many of the people I had served with. I cherished what I had learned about myself and the challenges that I had faced and overcome. But I hated being treated as a failure, even as I understood the stigma that stood in my way. I felt forced out, psychologically fractured. I had to get out to stay alive. My only option was to start all over again. The officer in charge of my premature voluntary release (PVR) signed off an email about me with more than a hint of sarcasm. Just under his signature block to my Commanding Officer he wrote, 'The caring, dedicated, compassionate Royal Logistic Corps Premature Voluntary Release Officer.' It hurt when I saw it. But over time, when you learn to care less about rank and promotion, they hold no power over you.

9

Motherhood

WE REMAINED LIVING on the base until my maternity leave ended. The Army provided the medical care I needed. At 37 weeks I went into labour. It was the middle of the night, and we were told to go straight to the hospital. A cheery-eyed doctor told me I was 8cm dilated and should be a mum by the morning, but 22 hours later my dream of a natural birth listening to whale music was off the agenda. When the nursing shift changed, the new midwife froze as she examined me. Our baby was in distress.

The room filled with people. Suddenly, there were forms to sign. Everything was moving faster and faster and I could hardly hear what was being said to me. The atmosphere in the operating theatre was cold and sterile. I searched anxiously for David's face. I was wheeled under a large white light. A big green sheet was hooked up to block the view of the lower half of my body. The anaesthetist rolled his stool to sit by my shoulder, gently tipping the table back and forth, asking if I could feel him touching my lower body. I was terrified that I would give the wrong answer.

David sat on the other side, his hands on my shoulder. I heard the sound as if ripping through fabric as they cut me open. The doctor peeked over the curtain and told me not to worry. I felt a tremendous weight on my stomach. It frightened me and I started to feel faint. I focused on the warmth of David's hand and soon heard the sound that I had been praying for – a strong, determined cry. The doctor lifted the baby over the curtain so I could see her. She was purple and puffy. I cried tears of relief. I could not believe she was my baby and that she had arrived safely.

She was 9lbs and we called her Bethan. The nurse swaddled her in a white blanket and handed her to David. I wanted to hold her, but was in no state to move my arms, so they brought her beautiful face closer to mine. David moved across to the other side of the room with her. He looked exhausted and slightly in shock. I lay there watching them, shaking uncontrollably.

I woke up to find David next to my bed. Beth was asleep in a cot. The nurse came to show me how to breastfeed. I was in pain. Even the simple task of sitting up in bed seemed impossible. So many cushions positioned to help me try to get comfortable. Then, no matter how I held Bethan, her mouth never positioned correctly. David tried to help. Everyone was tugging at me to get it right. A lactation specialist came in. I resented how easy and natural she made breastfeeding sound. I was delirious with frustration and fatigue. My body was failing and it was increasingly painful to even hold my baby. I started to get cold, then my wound started to ooze and my temperature kept rising. I had an infection.

Back at home on the base, David was incredible. He became a model father overnight. I watched him navigate visitors while changing nappies and taking phone calls. It was as if he had been doing it all his life. He tried to be light-hearted as he helped me move around the house, but I could not summon the energy to pretend everything was alright. David would help me to the sofa each morning with all the things I needed. He then left for work. He had already resigned his officer commission and was out working in the civilian world. When he came home, he found me exactly where he had left me. I felt trapped in the room and Beth would not stop crying. Both sets of grandparents came to see us, but when they visited I was desperate to give a good impression. The Army had hotwired it into me – you had to be tough to survive. We put a sign on the door asking for visitors to come back another time. I did not want anyone to see me like this.

The married quarters was not a particularly friendly place. All of our friends were still single and lived in the Officers' Mess and the neighbours were of a higher rank. I was relieved when we finally drove away.

In the blink of an eye, I was on the other side.

When you leave the Army, everything cuts off. David and I were isolated and alone. We had not just lost our jobs, we had lost our home, our friends and the community in which we lived. We had also lost contact with the friends we had had before the Army. I kept my family at a distance. We had to start all over again.

Life as a new mum was not what I had imagined. I had swapped a highly disciplined environment for life with a new-born baby that would not stop crying. Beth had terrible colic and we tried everything to console her – rocking her gently, warm baths. We even took her to a cranial osteopath, but nothing seemed to help. Everything was completely overwhelming.

We bought a new build property in what turned out to be a rough part of High Wycombe, west of London. There was an alleyway at the back of the house. Local youths hung out there hurling stones and verbal abuse over the fence. I felt constantly under threat and kept a knife next to my bed. It was the only way I could fall asleep. It gave me a sense of agency and of being in control. As I pushed the pram down the street, I would clock each parked car, each person around me, checking who came and went. It felt important for me to be ready for anything at any time. Even a car backfiring or a door slamming would startle me and make me dive for cover.

I was the product of a masculine culture that did not tolerate femininity. I had adapted my identity and my behaviour to be accepted as one of the guys. I had had to prove myself by using the parts of my identity that made me 'not like other girls'. Behaving like the men, demonstrating my physical strength and hiding my vulnerability, was the only way to survive. Motherhood required an entirely new set of skills that they do not teach you in the Army. Outside of the wire, my behaviour and my leadership style violated given stereotypes. I was deemed too abrupt, too aggressive, too forthright. Everything the Army had taught me was now considered too masculine for civilian life. As a woman I was somehow expected to show a more refined, softer, more delicate side. I told myself that I needed to stop swearing, to stop yelling so much and adjust my scowling expression. The additional layer of trying to hide my mental illness turned me into a pressure cooker. I was holding on too tight. Standing on the edge, spinning in no-man's land.

I still had rages. Once my parents had Beth for a day and when I went to collect her they had put a stair gate across the kitchen door to stop the dog getting out. I was on edge – it took just one critical comment to trigger me. There was no warning, I ripped the stair gate off the door and started raging. My mother was holding Beth, cowering on the stairs as I stood over her, fist clenched and screaming. I was threatening and abusive. I remember the spittle from my mouth hitting my mother's face as she sat on the stairs shielding Beth. My mother was clearly frightened of me.

I joined mums' group coffee mornings, but just felt awkward – the acceptable language, the dress code and the humour were different. I tried to conceal my veteran status because I needed to fit in with the other mums. I was not interested in baby talk. I would still tie my shoelaces and tuck them into my boots like I did during service. I had no idea about makeup; there were no frills, no flowers or dresses in sight. I was afraid most of the time, but I tried to be present – to be the mother that I needed to be. Above all I wanted to be a good mum and up to the job.

We were short of money. It only added to the powder keg. I could not afford the price of a fancy coffee in the local café where the mother and baby group met up. I had a £10 a week budget for luxuries or socialising. David had had to take a job working for a pet nutrition company. He hated it and desperately missed his life in bomb disposal.

I was constantly exhausted. I did not realise it at the time, but on top of it all I had postnatal depression. Years later I would discover that the shift of hormones from pregnancy seemed to exacerbate my PTSD. The saving grace was that I returned to lacrosse training. As soon as David came back home in the evening, I would run off to the gym. It helped me to maintain an outward veneer of normality. I would plug in my headphones, the music loud, the beat strong, and push myself until I was exhausted, unable to think.

I began to feel increasingly restless. I looked for a community in veteran spaces, but most events amounted to a room full of men drinking pints and telling war stories. The charity sector grew, but events were largely marketed for the guys. Anything for women felt almost shrunk, joined up with military spouses, laced with pink camouflage and a free manicure on the side. There was no outlet and so I learned to stay quiet. On Remembrance Sunday, I felt invisible. The assumption was that I was there to support David's former life. I never wore my medals. It was partly out of anger, but I was also ashamed that I only had two to show for my brief career. There were periods of stability where

I would cope and seem normal to those around me. I would cook meals, socialise and laugh, but the despair was always waiting quietly to catch me. As my anger and resentment simmered, I would pay a heavy price for my silence.

There was no medical aftercare provided by the Army, so we turned to the NHS. I was put back on anti-depressants after I stopped breastfeeding. The staff had little experience of treating veterans – let alone female veterans. In 2004, when Bethan was two, I saw a consultant psychiatrist privately. He was kind and patient, diagnosing me with PTSD. He gently suggested a course of Cognitive Behavioural Therapy, but my mind was spinning and I struggled to hear or recall what he was saying to me. I was there in his office, but fading in and out of his sentences. Panic built inside of me at the idea of re-exposing myself in therapy after my experience in the Army. I left his office, back in control, but pushing aside everything he had said to me.

At this point I was still a full-time mum, looking after Beth and training for the next lacrosse World Cup. We always hoped that we would have another baby and that schedule was timetabled by my lacrosse commitments. I had just played in the 2005 World Cup and there was this self-imposed urgency to get pregnant, have a baby and get fit again before the 2009 World Cup. David and I left Bethan with his parents and went on holiday to Egypt, where we started trying.

We moved three times in three years. After a year in High Wycombe, we moved to a cottage in Marlow. It was lovely, but too small for another baby. By the time we moved to Reigate to be closer to my parents in 2006, I was heavily pregnant. David was away working in Afghanistan as a civilian contractor. I was left in the new house looking after Bethan. We had agreed the purchase on probate, so the house was still full of the previous owner's possessions. I was surrounded by stacks of unpacked cardboard boxes. They were too heavy for me to move, so they sat half-opened in the corridors and bedrooms. I could not find a single thing. There was no cooker, so I rustled up dinner on a camping stove and in the microwave. I had come off the anti-depressants while I was pregnant and in the last few months my mood began to dip.

The doctors agreed I could have a natural birth. When my contractions started at 41 weeks everything went at breakneck speed. When we arrived at the hospital, I was taken straight into the labour room. Then the baby got stuck. I remember looking down at his head between my legs, hearing the midwife shouting at me to stop pushing. His shoulder was stuck behind my pubic bone, preventing the birth of his body. A red light started flashing and more people arrived in the room. It was excruciatingly painful. I was badly torn but had a beautiful baby boy called Tom, who was 9lbs just like his sister. Not long after, I caught Strep B, which meant that Tom had to have antibiotics every day. Within days, his bottom was like a blood orange and even the warmth of the bath could not soothe him.

I stayed at my parents' house as David was away with work. The midwife came to check how I was healing, but the tear got infected and needed further treatment.

I was so sore that, for weeks, I could only sit down on a square cushion with a hole in the middle. I was left feeling lost, angry, rebellious and sad. I was convinced I was a bad mother. I was a biff, a total failure for a second time. I withdrew into myself. When Tom was three months old, I stopped seeing people. Eventually I stopped going out altogether and did not even bother to answer the phone. Soon friends and family stopped calling, unaware of the disaster capsizing our lives.

Feeling cast out and isolated, life became inconsolably desperate. I became more and more fearful of being ignored or abandoned. The pain had to find another outlet. I found myself consumed by a primitive, almost volcanic and explosive rage. I started arguing about the tiniest, most irrelevant things. My behaviour became increasingly irrational. I flew into rages and would lock myself in the bathroom, afraid of losing control around my children, screaming and shouting at anything before dissolving into heaving sobs. Beth would bring me a box of tissues as the dust settled. David had returned, and would explain to her that Mummy was just tired. But it took its toll – Beth started to twist her hair around her finger until it came out in chunks. Tom would not stop crying. His rages had an uncanny resemblance to mine.

I had invested so much in the image of myself as a soldier – invincible and strong. I had been taught to hide any sense of weakness or vulnerability, but it was not holding together anymore. All of my unfinished business was now on public display and the reflection was something that I was unwilling and unprepared to acknowledge. It was humiliating and it hurt like nothing else had ever done before. I was so deeply invested in what I had been taught to be that I grappled to regain it. I needed it to confirm who I was, to congratulate me and make me feel completely whole. I could not, I would not, confront my fear because I needed to be seen as perfect and in control.

My failure to be the ideal soldier became a deep and consuming source of shame. I could not address it, feel it or tolerate it. I lost connection with everything and everyone. Who I was and my place in the world became facts that I could no longer recall. I feared rejection from others, so I cut myself off and purposefully caged the need to belong. Beyond being a soldier, I had no way to embrace my fears or to acknowledge my vulnerabilities. And then, my failure to mother and to conform to what was demanded of me began to crush what fragile reserves I had left. I internalised it all, assuming that something was fundamentally wrong with me. I was left silently screaming and reaching for the next hit, the next vacuous high. On bad nights I lay awake, ruminating over my failure. Should I have stayed in? … if only I had gone back? … maybe I would have had a chance to right my wrongs?

Then I began to drag David down with me. In a violent rage, I locked myself in the bedroom. He broke down the door and forced me to the floor. I screamed, I cried and yelled incoherent expletives, but he restrained me, he held me, until I was too exhausted to fight. Clearing up the broken pictures and repairing holes in the walls became a part of daily life. It was completely irrational that I would want to push away the person that showed me so much love, that I would subject our children, whom I love so deeply, to witness such terror, sadness and pain. It would take all my strength to keep it contained during the day and then in the evening it would erupt like a fault line.

I began to think about suicide. Imagining it gave me a sense of relief. I just had to stop everything. I was hurting my husband and I could not protect my own children from the feelings that were raging inside of me. I started drinking again. I drove the car as fast as I could, hoping fate would make the decision for me.

10

Dogs and Helicopters

IN CRISIS, DAVID resorted to private care. I simply could not wait six to eight weeks for an appointment on the NHS. On the internet he found Dr Adrian Gillham, a former military psychiatrist who worked at the Priory in Surrey. Just before Christmas 2006, Dr Gillham diagnosed me, this time with severe PTSD directly attributable to my military service. By now, I was so ill that I had no choice but to finally hear the words and accept them. It was as if a weight had been lifted. The dots were now joined and the seriousness of my mental health was acknowledged and assigned to the cause. There was actually something medically wrong with me and it was not my fault, but by the time the new year dawned I was so ill that he advised that I was admitted to the Priory for a course of treatment. As I packed my bag, I felt an overwhelming sense of relief. I did not have to pretend anymore, but I will never forget the children's faces as I waved them goodbye. From now on, I could only see them under supervision. I was too numb to feel anything.

The Priory was a large white country house surrounded by gardens on the edge of a village near Woking in Surrey. A long driveway led up to the front door. Inside, it looked like a country house hotel. The only giveaways were the nurses in uniform and the dazed looking patients. A winding staircase with an oak banister led upstairs to the rooms. Mine was at the end of the corridor. It had white walls, a single bed, a chair and a desk. It was completely sanitised and there were no hooks in case you tried to hang yourself. There was no way out either. The sash window that overlooked the garden did not fully open. There was a white bar across the top part of the glass.

There were endless forms to sign. A nurse checked my bags and clothes. I did not fight it because, for the first time in ages, I felt safe, safe from myself. Being in a mental hospital meant I could stop smiling. I did not have to talk to anyone. In the canteen I would eat eyes down, pretending not to see the other patients around me. I could just take the medication and shut down. As the days went by, I became increasingly selfish. I stopped caring about life outside and the people who loved me.

The list of medication was endless: Trazodone, Clonazepam, Fluoxetine, Chlorpromazine, Escitalopram, Citalopram, Amitriptyline, Pregabalin, Lorazepam and Zopiclone – all flooding through me one after the other. When one didn't work, they would stop it and try another. My appetite disappeared and I could no longer go running, one of the few releases I had left. I was plagued with crippling stomach pains, a dry mouth and a persistent headache. The idea of taking medication to deal with my head scared me, but I was too tired to fight it.

Heavily medicated, life took on a welcome haze. The rage faded in a sedated fog. I succumbed to the dead weight of tranquillisers to get me through the day and sleeping pills at night. I chain-smoked. Every fifteen minutes a nurse would pop her head around the door to check on me. When the bell rang, I lined up with the other patients in the downstairs corridor. A nurse would appear in a hatch on the opposite side of the wall. One by one we were called forward and presented with a small, white paper container with tablets. It was always the same routine – swallowing the pills and then sticking out my tongue to prove there was nothing left inside my mouth.

Soon, I found myself drifting through the day, lumbering and unable to walk up the stairs unaided. I began hearing people as if they were talking to me from a distance. I hit a stage of apathy where I just did not care about what happened next, a kind of emotional death. In a psychiatric hospital, not many friends come and visit or bring you grapes. The corridors whisper this deafening roar of rejection. The stigma is humiliating, but the silence is suffocating. The screams of the young girl down the corridor when her family came to visit and the sound of the Army firing range in the distance were the only things that would jolt me to my senses.

After the PTSD diagnosis, a tsunami of therapy sessions followed. The day began at 9am sharp and went on until 5pm. The Lodge, where we went for therapy, was on the other side of the driveway and I was escorted across the lawns. I had to sign in and out to be allowed to leave the main building. The problem was that, at the time, the Priory had little experience of dealing with military trauma despite the fact that Dr Gillham was himself a veteran.

There were rounds of Cognitive Behavioural Therapy. It is a method that tries to change the way you think about something so that you can eventually view it through a different lens. It challenges your thoughts, core beliefs, automatic thoughts or distorted patterns, replacing them with more helpful ways of seeing things. It is a method that relies on rational thinking and so is completely useless in the middle of a flashback or anxiety attack, when only an Olympian feat of rational thought could deal with it.

In Art Therapy we were told to paint and draw what we were feeling. I am no artist, but was often surprised what ended up on the paper in front of me. One session, I was presented with a circular outline of a face and a pot of paints. I picked up some scissors and cut a zigzag through the head, then took a thick brush and painted a red line across it. I just sat looking at it for the rest of the session.

Drama Therapy was extremely uncomfortable. I hated acting out my experiences and turning the people in my dreams into characters. It felt ridiculous, belittling and demeaning. It gave no value to the lives of the people in my dreams. Another veteran had joined the group. He lashed out and shouted at the therapist. He said she had no idea what he had been through. When he first spoke up, I cried uncontrollably. His words were my words. Hearing my thoughts put into words by another human being simply overwhelmed me. To find someone who shared a similar experience, someone who understood, somehow validated my pain. The danger was that our shared experience would develop into something more between us. We were two vulnerable people looking to escape. At my lowest, it was tempting to torch everything, the connection was so powerful. It would have been so easy to escape into it, but my love for David stopped me.

In Eye Movement Desensitisation and Reprocessing, EMDR, I was taught to move my eyes in a specific way in order to process the trauma. It is gut-wrenching and visceral. Although it did not heal me, it began to allow me to reconsider the memories in a safer way rather than simply avoiding them. I would sit right in front of the therapist as she asked me to describe the ambush and the woman in the red wellington boots, painting unsavoury images with harrowing clarity. She would ask me to follow her finger, moving it from side to side in front of my eyes, and then encourage me to turn the pulsating colours into black and white, to turn down the sounds and alter the smells that engulfed me. One image would resurrect and then trigger another, each one revealed with nauseating lucidity. The panic would come and I would struggle to speak. When the memories overwhelmed me, she would bring me back to my 'safe place' and urge me to breathe deeply. I left each session feeling dazed, as if marginally removed from my body. There was a small toilet at the bottom of the stairs near the back door of the hospital. I would lock myself in and taste my vomit rising. I broke down, shaking and dry heaving. Over time, I began gagging instinctively, purging the paralysing pictures inside me. Then I would sit hunched on the floor, the door still locked, gathering the strength to step outside.

Then came Narrative Therapy, which involves writing down your story and then sharing it with others. The aim is to externalise what has happened and share it. The writing was helpful. It was hard, but there was something cathartic about picking up a pen and committing the past to paper. Bringing the past back to life seemed indulgent and scary; it left me exhausted, but it helped. It was, in many ways, the beginning of this book, but verbally articulating my words in a group setting felt impossible. I was the only veteran in the narrative group and my story was very different from theirs.

One morning, I felt strong enough to read aloud a scene from Kosovo. But I wish I hadn't. It was a graphic account of what I had seen at the white car ambush. As I spoke, I could feel that my description repelled and alienated those in the circle around me. My story was so far removed from anything they had experienced. It was unpalatable. Normally, PTSD is triggered by one event, but I had a myriad of memories that overwhelmed me. Unintentionally, it created a hierarchy of trauma where others felt unwilling to share. In turn, I became more reluctant to engage for fear of becoming the problem and stifling other people's recovery. In the confines of group therapy, it is difficult to hide anger. I would hold on for as long as politely possible and then explode.

belligerently. I shouted, swore and became aggressive. The other patients watched me, stunned. It was decided that I should no longer be part of the group, but focus on 1:1 therapy.

I spent my weeks bouncing from one session to another. It smothered my hopeless negativity, filling every available moment with something, forcing me to keep focused and purposefully busy, but on top of the increasing dose of medication it was toxic and ripped open Pandora's box. The therapists had no idea of how to put the lid back on. They were constantly switching my medication, changing the therapy and the therapists, trying something new. I was left totally disorientated.

David brought Tom to the hospital, but I was too nervous to hold him and appeared detached. I was frightened that I could not take care of him. The longer I stayed in, the harder it became to think of starting over outside. It was easier inside. Shut away, I had no need to pretend.

My behaviour became increasingly delusional, dysfunctional and irrational. They were trying to help me, but I started to fight against it. Then I added alcohol to the mix for good measure. I used my military training to escape to the pub each night. Looking back, I am mortified at my defiance, crawling in the grass to avoid the security lights. I could hear the sergeant's voice ringing in my ears to get down on my 'belt buckle' and 'zigzag' out of sight. I created a scenario in my head that people were looking for me. In the pub, I would study entry and exit points ahead of time, rotating from pub to pub and using a different 'movement order' each night. I always sat in the corner, pint in hand watching the door. Always ready, scanning everyone who came in and out and at precisely what time. I chased the warm wash of relief and felt my body loosen. It worked like nothing else, but I became abusive towards those who were trying to help me. It just felt easier to push everyone away. My desire to self-destruct was on overdrive.

Then the money ran out. My medical insurance covered the first four weeks, but I was not ready to go home. David tried to borrow money, but people were reluctant to help. My father stepped in to pay for two more weeks, but then the pot ran dry. So I continued my treatment as an outpatient, driving in to the hospital daily.

There were nights when I chose to sleep rough, outside in the elements. I had a warm bed at home, but even there I could not face the world and I did not want the world to see me. I took one step forward and then two steps back. There were days when I needed to escape from everything. David knew I was sleeping rough. He rationalised that I was going to do it anyway, however much he protested, so he just made sure that I had what I needed. When I went back to the Priory for therapy, I would always take my rucksack, complete with sleeping bag and small stove. I had everything I required – warm jacket, cigarettes and my usual bottle of vodka tucked underneath my clothes. No-one ever found me, no-one knew where I was sleeping.

All I wanted in those long, relentless days was for it all to stop, but there was no end to it. There was no finish line. I stopped living for the future and as such everything became provisional. Days appeared unfading, filled with apathy and despondent fatigue. In my mind, my life was over and done with. Everything outside felt remote – out of reach. I became increasingly detached, as if looking on from another world. I could not escape from looking at the past, but in doing so the present became pointless and the future non-existent.

There was a summer house in the Priory grounds where I would sit for hours, thinking. Sometimes I would go there at night and sleep on the benches, wrapped in anything I could find to protect myself from the February cold. It felt good to be alone, away from everyone and unaccountable. One afternoon, as I sat in the summer house waiting for my appointment with the psychiatrist, I pulled out a knife from the top pocket in my rucksack. I felt an empty despair unlike anything I had experienced before. My mind loomed vacant, somehow removed from my body. There was no energy behind the emotion, just methodical intent with the sole purpose of escaping from it. I opened the blade and rolled up my left sleeve to expose a wrist. It did not feel like my body, it did not look like my skin. The knife was not as sharp as I would have liked. David had switched my favourite Leatherman for a blunt blade. Nevertheless, I persisted. I cut again and again until the blood started to seep. Relief ran over my skin.

It was as if I was a bystander, observing from a distance. There was no pain, there was no feeling. The blade moved in slow motion, as if my body was underwater, peacefully drowning. I rolled down my sleeve and watched my shirt absorb the blood. As I rolled up the other sleeve, a nurse appeared. He was carrying out routine checks around the building. His voice jolted me. It was caring and yet intrusive, but I did not want him to stop me. He took me to the psychiatrist's office and told him what he had seen. I felt no shame. His concern struck me as mildly amusing. The psychiatrist asked me to roll up my sleeves. In doing so, I launched into an assessment of how unsuccessful I had been. I even asked his advice on the angle of the incision. Bleeding from the wrists, I was defiantly calm, removed and belligerent.

The paramedics arrived and I was taken into another room. There were sidelong glances and scolding whispers. The psychiatrist came in with me. The paramedic was also a veteran and talked to him as if I was not there. He said scornfully that, in his opinion, 'I was only just out of nappies.' What I heard was that I was weak, that I had not done enough or seen enough to warrant my illness. What I heard was that I was a malingering attention seeker, a REMF, Rear Echelon Mother-Fucker. What right did I have to take up his time?

I pulled my hands away from him. The psychiatrist intervened, cajoling that we were both part of the same team. But it was too late. I was gone, running out of the building. The other patients stared, startled and even amused. Then I ran, faster and faster out of the main house, down the drive and into the woodland beyond the Lodge. I was consumed with panic. It pulsated through my body. I was convinced I was being abandoned again. Desperate and in despair, I escaped, zigzagging under the fence.

In the darkness I turned feral and downed a half-litre bottle of vodka. I did not dare smoke for fear of anyone seeing the light. Then I heard a sound all too familiar from military exercises – the distant hum of rotor blades. A helicopter was tracking me. The sound of the dogs soon followed, but by now I was in the stream, hoping to divert any scent, pleading that they would not find me. The dogs passed several times, straining on the leash, barking incessantly. I remained in the water, watching silently.

The helicopter lights turned towards me. I stood up slowly and walked towards the clearing. The dogs turned and ran straight at me. They threw me to the floor. As I covered my face, one Alsatian sank his teeth into me. It tore through my trousers, puncturing my skin. I could hardly feel the teeth. There was no anger, it meant nothing. The police asked me to tip out the contents of my pockets – cigarettes, tampons, the Lorazepam pills and a lighter were taken away. I was bundled into the back of an ambulance wet, cold, intoxicated and bleeding. I passed out. The police called David. He was working for a defence company as a business development manager and was in Abu Dhabi. It was his birthday. I don't remember if I spoke to him.

I woke up in a side room in A&E attached to a monitor that was sighing and bleeping. Wires pulled at my body as I lay on my back staring at the blank walls. Doctors came in and out at regular intervals armed with clip boards complete with forms and boxes to tick. Each one was cold, detached and condescending. They asked the same questions over and over. The same tone, the same antipathy. I struggle to recall how long it had been. The quantities of alcohol and prescription drugs I had consumed began to make the room spin, blurring my vision. Furious, I clawed at the clips and sensors, tearing them off. I opened the door of the room and ran through A&E, shouting at the people waiting patiently to see the doctor. No-one held my gaze – they all looked away from me. I had served my country and yet no-one cared. Why would they? I had no place in their lives. I felt betrayed and unworthy.

It was still dark outside the hospital. I walked, hugging the side of the pavement, for what seemed like an eternity. I looked destitute and was playing the role beautifully. I had lost my purse in the stream, so I had no money, and my mobile phone was out of battery. Hours passed. Then suddenly a taxi driver pulled up and wound down his window. He asked if I was alright and if I needed anything. I explained that I had no money, but that I needed a lift back to the Priory to find my things. I will never forget his kindness. He saved me that night and did not ask for anything. He helped me find my purse and made sure everything was alright before he left me. I will never forget the unconditional kindness and compassion of that stranger who took the time to notice, to care and to help me.

I went to therapy the next morning still wearing the same clothes, gargling mouthwash and chewing mints to kill off the smell, but fooling no-one. My wrists were bandaged. My leg was strapped. I sat there ashamed, unable to make eye-contact, motionless but breathing.

Not long after, I had a particularly difficult EMDR session. David was away working, so it was decided that I should stay at my parents' house for a few days rather than be alone with the children. His mother looked after Beth and Tom in our family home a few streets away. After the session, I drove back to Reigate and went for a drink to decompress. My parents called up to find out where I was and were angry to hear that I was in a pub. My brother phoned and said I was being selfish and hurting the family. He added it was time to grow up and take responsibility, but his anger simply emboldened my drinking. Eventually, my sister arrived and took me home to sleep on her sofa. The next day, when I went back to my parents' house, I found all my belongings by the roadside at the end of the driveway. The gates were locked. I picked up what I could and disappeared. I understand their frustration, but I didn't have the energy to deal with them. It was easier to shut down my emotions and walk away.

David came back from working abroad, he found me and took me home. Bethan was only five years old. She smothered me with her warm hugs and kisses. Tom was beautiful too, so many gurgling smiles and raspberry blowing giggles as we played on the floor. He was just nine months old, but I am not even sure he recognised me as his mother. He had changed so much, I felt like an add-on as I tried to settle him for bed. He refused to take his milk from me. He pulled away and cried. I was heartbroken as I watched David take over. Tom curled up in his arms and fell asleep. I got angry with Beth when all I wanted to do was cuddle her. Her behaviour was understandably challenging, but I should have just held her and made up for lost time. Even making love with David felt so different. I longed to be with him, but my body felt numb and distant.

The way people reacted to me changed dramatically. Some wanted to 'fix me', told me to pull myself together and that it was 'all in my head.' Others shunned me like a leper. No wonder, I had become cynical and reckless, lacking the energy to remain polite.

One day after a session of EMDR, I decided to sleep in my usual hideaway up a disused stairwell behind the hospital. I set up for the night under the second-floor platform with a bottle of vodka. I slipped into my green army sleeping bag, but awoke within hours. I sat bolt upright, startled, fear gripping every sinew. As is still the case now, when the nightmares come I am too frightened to close my eyes, yet, exhausted, I long for sleep, for a moment of respite. The vodka bottle was empty, so I searched for something else, reeling, reckless, spinning in a desperate desire to escape and destroy the images running through my mind as a blinding fury consumed me. There were some blue Lorazepam pills in my pocket, but not enough to sedate me. Hunting for more, I found two first aid kits in the front pocket of my rucksack – army issue, still wrapped in their green plastic. I peeled open the first and then the second and knocked back the white pills. I am not sure how many, it did not matter. I waited for the numbness. And then I was gone. Sleep soon came.

At daybreak I awoke unsteady. It was difficult to

breathe. My vision was distorted and blurred. I stumbled down the metal steps and rushed into the hospital toilet. I locked the door, still dressed in my army green Buffalo jacket and warm hat. Hours later, I came round lying on the floor, languishing in my own urine. My skin was cold and clammy, my hands jittering. I managed to call David, punching the buttons on my phone slowly. I staggered to my feet and slipped out of the hospital through the smoking room and into the car park at the back of the building. David found me delirious by the roadside, choking on my own vomit. The pills were morphine.

David took me home and called A&E. I could hear the exasperation in his voice as he talked to the doctors. The children were in the sitting room just looking at me silently. It was a turning point. I saw the hurt and the pain I was causing. How I was damaging those people who loved me. My parents had kicked me out. My siblings no longer spoke to me. My friends had stopped calling. But David was still there, loving me unconditionally. As I looked at our children, I knew they needed a mother and I had to get better for them.

11

No Man's Land

AFTER I WAS diagnosed with PTSD, I had to deal with the stigma, which was more debilitating than the illness itself. For years, its grip stifled and imprisoned me. I was frightened I would never be good enough again. I was left numb, isolated, anxious, fragile and sad. I emerged on the other side more resilient, but as vulnerable as ever.

We are encouraged to speak of mental illness in the same way as we talk about physical illness, but I can assure you that having PTSD is nothing like a broken arm. Military training is physically damaging, and as a result I have had surgery on various parts of my body, but mental illness is nothing like it. My ankle reconstruction did not cause me to behave erratically. Hip surgery did not make me lash out at family and friends. Elbow surgery did not urge me to end everything. The truth is that there is a wound and then there is all that emanates from it.

I had no solutions to my problems except those offered by others which were leading me into darker waters. I accepted and internalised the way other people saw me as a 'sufferer' and 'patient.' I took the drugs they handed to me which produced symptoms that looked and felt like the madness they were meant to be healing. It was less easy to confront the human failure that I felt – this deep-rooted feeling that I should have done something to prevent the disaster that had engulfed not just me, but also my family.

There was no click of a switch and I was suddenly better.

In the months that followed, my time was still structured by therapy sessions and doses of medication in the morning and evening. It was a slow process of finding a routine again, starting with setting an alarm to get out of bed each morning, taking a shower and getting dressed. As David went back to work, I had to step up and look after the children. It helped kick-start the routine, as I had no choice. I had to take some responsibility again. We would agree what we were going to eat each evening, so I had a plan of what to cook – it made me eat properly again, made me start to look after myself. I still did not have the energy to exercise, or even the inclination. My goal each day was to simply get out of the house. Beth was at pre-school, so I would walk with Tom to collect her. I would skulk at the edge of the playground waiting for her to come out, or sometimes pretend that I was on the telephone so no-one would talk to me. At first, Beth went to my old school – I could not face the same teachers. I did not want them to see me this way or have to explain. At school I had been the strong, successful sportswoman – now I looked a mess. Some days, speaking to other people just required too much energy and I would wear my headphones as a sign to others to 'go away!'.

Towards the end of 2007, I took a job in London as a leadership consultant. Leadership was what I knew, converting my practical military training and experience into a business setting. It seemed like a natural fit. I would need to develop my commercial understanding, but Sandhurst was still considered to be a world-leading leadership academy. It gave me instant credibility. I spent three nights a week away from home running residential client workshops. I did it to stop the noise, focusing my mind on something other than the repetitive and negative audio in my head. It forced a routine on me. I had to get up and look smart, put on a metaphorical mask and face the world. It forced the transition from the hospital to the real world, but as ever I was taking things at a sprint, pushing myself to the extreme.

I spent 18 months at the firm until one of the directors refused my request for a few hours' leave. I wanted to see Beth in her first Nativity play. He was an old-school misogynist. His language was derogatory and demeaning. Everyone knew that his behaviour was unacceptable, but no-one said anything. He was the type of character that would insist you stayed in the bar drinking with him until the early hours of the morning. He refused my request and told me that I needed to learn to set the example. He wanted me present at all times, even when not required for delivering a session. I lost my temper. My response was disproportionate, triggered by unhelpful memories. I was called in to see the Managing

Director. He was sympathetic, but also protective of his colleague. Emails were circulated back and forth, all positioning to protect him. I felt 'othered' again while the Board protected his unacceptable behaviour, making excuses for him. This was a man who chased down clients who had shared unfavourable feedback. A man that other women in the business had asked not to work with. But no-one on the Board said anything. I spoke to Dr Gillham, who put me on two weeks' sick leave. I resigned. I simply could not face working amidst the duplicity.

My regular therapist left the Priory and so I started to see another clinical psychologist privately. I would travel to her house in Guildford for sessions every fortnight. She continued the EMDR work that the Priory had started. Long periods followed when I simply took medication and sometimes I was completely free of the regime of pill-taking. Then a trigger would set everything off again. It could be a story or a set of images on the news. Often it was simply because I was exhausted pretending everything was fine. It did not help that David was made redundant suddenly.

Our financial pressures were building and we ran out of funds to keep paying for private treatment. So, in 2008, Dr Gillham arranged for me to have some remedial treatment through the charity Combat Stress. I was admitted to Tyrwhitt House treatment centre in Leatherhead for two weeks. My stay was paid for by the Service Personnel and Veterans Agency, founded in 2007 as an executive agency of the UK Ministry of Defence providing support to veterans. Combat Stress was founded in the immediate aftermath of the First World War in 1919, and for years it was the only charity that specialised in caring for veterans with mental health difficulties. Tyrwhitt House is a large country house with spacious grounds, not dissimilar to the Priory. It had 30 single bedrooms, with veterans staying for one to three weeks at a time.

I parked on the sweeping gravel drive and walked into the reception nervously. A bald-headed ex-soldier approached me. He had the standard issue military tattoos down both arms, biceps bulging. In any other setting he might have seemed threatening, but he came right over, placed his hand on my arm and welcomed me. He told me not to worry, that we were all in there for the same thing. That everyone was here to help. His warmth and kindness immediately settled me.

My needs were then assessed by the nursing staff and a treatment plan was agreed. There was a program of arts and crafts activities, and outings were arranged, but everything was relaxed, less onerous than the Priory. I spent many hours just walking and sitting with other veterans. It felt safe, I felt validated, I could breathe again. Being amongst other veterans who understood was powerfully healing.

I started playing lacrosse again. I am not sure why, but I struggled to let go of it. Perhaps I was trying to reclaim a piece of my identity. I was struggling to get fit again, but went to the European Games in Lahti, Finland, as part of the B team. There was, however, nothing left in the tank either physically or emotionally. There were tensions between myself and my teammates.

It was as if a dark cloud was hanging over me. Being on tour away from home and having to share a room with someone else felt suffocating. There was nowhere to be alone and stop pretending. I decided to fly home midway through the tournament. Lacrosse had been such a huge part of my life, but I was now a very different version of the person that I used to be. It was the end of an era and it was heart-wrenching.

I asked to go back to Tyrwhitt House for another period of respite, but their waiting lists were too long. After operations in Iraq and Afghanistan, hundreds of British veterans were now waiting for care and Combat Stress was completely overstretched. Then Dr Gillham retired and referred me back to the NHS.

In an endless cycle, I have spent more than 20 years in and out of psychiatric clinics, being fed mind-numbing, brightly coloured pills. Decades spent with therapists, embracing valiant efforts to seek a more objective truth. Years spent living under the psychiatric gaze. The onset of a bout of illness is always the same. I feel adrift, unable to keep up. It is marked by irritability and insomnia. I start a sentence and forget its ending. I feel frightened, alone and disoriented.

The pills have allowed me to breathe in the short term, but the withdrawal process is debilitating. Each time, disabled by symptoms so similar to the illness itself, I have either been advised to increase the dosage or to continue taking the pills for the rest of my life. For me, the side effects subtract from life, making life feel like a journey in the middle lane of a motorway – neither fast nor slow. Somehow, by numbing the desperate lows, they also steal the joy-giving highs. It is as if they remove an essential part of me as a human being. The numbing fog is a life-saving distraction, but sometimes the prospect of eternal dependence can feel like a hopeless story, trapped and void of all feeling.

I returned to Cognitive Behavioural Therapy (CBT) for years as it is the therapy that the NHS tend to rely on, the default option, but it never touched my trauma. It was impossible to reorganise the memories into a logical, conscious narrative. Instead, they would leak out at unbearable moments, triggered by a set of emotions that I struggled to consciously express. I would enter fight, flight or freeze mode every single time. I question whether so much of my thinking was indeed such a distorted representation of reality. Everything I did, said and thought was judged and evaluated through the prism of the CBT value system. Worse, I had begun to adopt the same gaze myself. I had learned to monitor and alter my thoughts and actions according to what psychiatry deemed to be appropriate and correct, or, to use their language, 'healthy'. My thoughts were unpleasant and at times unbearable, but the positive alternative that my therapist suggested reflected a naïve and biased grasp of what was actually happening. The simple truth is that some of what happened was indeed my fault, my responsibility, and by taking refuge in positive clichés I just created further disillusionment. I did not need to be healed with CBT to become more realistic. The problem was that I had seen the truth and the experience had shattered my existing perspective. It had destroyed the rules and foundations upon which I had formerly made sense of my life. Each time I left an appointment, I would walk out more tearful, more defiant and more desperate than the last time.

I began to hate the system, hate its ineptitude and incapacity. Being asked the same questions again and again by countless professionals. Repeating my story over and over in an endless quest to find someone who could treat me. I hated being asked to fill out a myriad of forms to access a service, only to be told that I was on a waiting list for a year. Being matched with a therapy or therapist that was unsuitable, or struggling to secure a ten-minute appointment to see my GP. I hated the trial and error of finding a medication that worked, being told that it is necessary by one doctor and then that it is wrong by another. It turned me into a cynic, questioning if the professionals actually knew what they were doing. I lost faith in the system as I became increasingly desperate. I began to believe that nobody could help me and the unbearable situation I had found myself in was fixed for life.

In 2009, I joined Cable and Wireless Worldwide as a Talent and Leadership Development Manager. I had managed their account whilst working for the previous consultancy and they had head hunted me. I was drawn to help other people be the best that they could be. After so many years of soul searching, I was intrigued by the human condition and the impact that leaders can have on our performance and wellbeing. But I was also compelled by a need to achieve something again. Propelling myself forwards was somehow more comfortable than staying frozen with fear. Being busy and in control helped to calm the worry that still invaded every part of me. I became obsessive over small details in an attempt to take control and calm my racing thoughts. I excelled at the job, partly due to my experience and credibility, but also because of a tendency towards perfectionism and overthinking. I was high-functioning and high-achieving, asking 'what if?' of everything. I would arrive early for work, always prepared, never missing a deadline or falling short in any aspect of delivery. My superpower became my hypervigilance, my ability to read a room and pick up on the smallest of cues. I could not turn it off or put it on pause because it hid this constant churn of anxiety. Ironically, it was the nervous energy that kept me going, this fear of failing.

It was a long commute every day on the M25. We had an au pair to look after the children, but I rarely saw them before bedtime in the week. I felt conflicted between forging a new career and missing out on my children and family. I would arrive back home in the evenings more and more depleted. But back in the office, no-one saw through me. It lasted for 18 months, until I couldn't hold up the mask any longer. I was exhausted in my mind and body. Being apart from my family left me with conflicting values. I reduced my workload, but it was still not enough to renew my energy.

In 2010, I set up my own business in leadership development and coaching. I needed the flexibility to be able to manage my health more proactively. My perfectionist approach did not change very much, it was still extremely high-functioning, but it allowed me greater control and the freedom to rest and recharge when necessary. It blessed me with more time for my family. I'd also launched in the build-up to the 2012 London Olympic and Paralympic Games, which meant there was work available that aligned perfectly with my skill set. My client base grew helping Great Britain's teams prepare for a home games and before long I was consulting with large corporations again. Even so, I could not ignore a nagging voice urging me to try again for another baby. I wanted the opportunity to get it right this time and be a better mother third time round. I had this idea that I could do it better and be able to relax and enjoy motherhood. It was far from rational, more of an unconscious need. David was more cautious. He was worried about my health and the risks of another difficult labour. Reluctant at first, he eventually agreed and we decided to start trying.

James was born in November 2011. Like his brother and sister, he was 9lbs. It was considered a high-risk pregnancy, so I was under consultant care. They had strongly advised me to have a planned c-section and I agreed. I just wanted a healthy baby and to minimise the risks. The idea of a natural birth seemed completely irrelevant. The c-section was booked for week 39.

I was in and out of the maternity ward in the weeks leading up to the delivery with several false labours. Then, on the weekend before the planned c-section, it started properly. There was no room in the operating theatre and so they allowed me to progress naturally. The nightmare started all over again, with hours of labour, James distressed and no end in sight. We were left in a side room until a midwife came in and said that she had not realised we were in there as the handover had not been properly completed. She took one look at me and called in the doctor. Once again, the room filled with people and consent forms were pushed in front of me.

I had had no medication besides gas and air and was exhausted. People kept drifting in and out of my vision. Once in theatre, the midwife tried to move James' position. He was the wrong way around, head down but with his back against my back and had stopped progressing. I was on my back, my feet fixed in stirrups and her hands inside me. More people came in. The anaesthetist sat next to my shoulder starting to prep me. A female consultant arrived and took control. I don't remember making any sound as she turned James, but the pain was indescribable. It is an agony that I still struggle to fully connect with today. I dragged on the face-mask, biting down on the mouth piece to try and find some relief. David squeezed my hand. I could feel his fear and sense of helplessness. I have no memory of holding James immediately afterwards. They had to stretcher me off the table. Then I was wheeled down the corridor to recover. James was swaddled and sleeping.

David left to collect Beth and Tom early from school. The head teacher went into their classroom to tell them they had a new baby brother. It was pouring with rain, and they arrived at the hospital drenched but excited. I could hear Beth outside the room, resisting her father's attempts to brush her hair and make her look presentable. Tom perched next to me on the bed as they wheeled us around to the main ward. Beth walked alongside, holding her daddy's hand. I felt a huge sense of relief, grateful that James was safe and healthy.

I suffered a prolapse with bladder difficulties as a result. Attending my first physiotherapist appointment, I had expected the usual sports rehabilitation routine and was shocked to have her put on her gloves and examine me. It took months of recovery to be able to go to the toilet normally and even more time before I could so much as think about lifting weights or running. But eventually I started exercising again, albeit slowly.

In 2013 we moved from Surrey to the Welsh borders. I wanted a fresh start. David also wanted to get away from everything. We wanted to put distance between us and what had happened. I needed to move away, to start again where no-one really knew me. Bethan was about to start secondary school, I was running my own business and David's job was home based, so we had no need to be near London any longer. We found a converted barn in the country surrounded by beautiful fields and green space. The Brecon Beacons and the River Wye were on our doorstep. The children adapted quickly to their new schools and friendship groups. I was immeasurably grateful. It felt like we could breathe again.

At times, my reactions were still disproportionate. James running into the kitchen and pointing a plastic toy pistol in my direction would make me shout. Tom coming around the corner unexpectedly would make me swear and the children recoil. A bone of contention had always been Bonfire Night. The undeniable irony was that David still loved doctoring loud bangs and explosions; it gave him an exhilarating high. Each year, he would plan displays of increasing magnitude for the children to enjoy, but for me it felt impossible to relax. Anxiety magnifies the significance of everything – every little spark, every ember of light. Over the years, I have found ways of engaging for the sake of the kids – I run around keeping busy with a drink in hand, trying to disguise the fact that I am unravelling. Rationally, I understand the difference between fireworks and bullets, but I seem unable to filter my instinctive fear.

As a small child, Tom was deemed to have behavioural problems and I felt guilty. I was convinced that it was my fault. It stemmed from the fact that he had pronounced speech difficulties and would get frustrated as few people could understand him. At nursery, he struggled to manage his anger and I would be called in almost daily. The buxom supervisor would beckon me over from the school gate and express her sullen disappointment. Tom, she said, refused to conform, he would not stand in line. Once he became so frustrated that he stabbed another child in the hand with a pair of school scissors. Thankfully, they were blunt, but I blamed myself and believed my trauma had damaged him. When we moved to Monmouthshire, I was terrified of the first parents' evening, willing my child to be accepted and liked in his new school. Waiting in line, his French teacher, Madame Le Mole, invited me to join her. She smiled and described what a wonderful and kind boy Tom is. As she spoke, I started crying, overwhelmed by her generous words and her warmth. I thanked her and raced straight out of the hall, hiding my face from the other parents. I sat alone in the car and started sobbing. They were tears of deep relief and pride. David had always said that I had never damaged the children and Madame Le Mole's kindness that day made me start to believe that they were going to be alright.

12

I Am (Invictus)

I THOUGHT I had forced myself to feel no attachment to the military, and instead had chosen to criticise it whenever I could. Clinging to an institution which was in every meaningful sense indifferent to me had been painfully demoralising and left me doubting my own worth. But Army training is more formative than you think – it shapes you in ways that you do not even realise at the time. I was no longer in the brotherhood, but the reality was, it was always in me. I tried to deny the fact that I still loved the military, because, at the same time, I hated it. Nevertheless, the ties ran deep and to my surprise, something happened to make me realise I still cared.

In January 2016, as I was reading the papers after dinner on a Sunday evening, I saw a small ad in *The Sunday Times* asking for wounded, injured and sick military veterans to audition to be part of a choir that TV personality Gareth Malone was putting together for the Invictus Games. As soon as I saw it, I knew I wanted to sing again. I did not think very much about the small print, which said that the BBC would be making a documentary about the choir. I submitted an audition video and was chosen. It gave me an opportunity to immerse myself once more in my old family and finally embrace the truth that I had a problem letting go.

The Invictus Games was set up by Prince Harry to harness the power of sport in assisting the rehabilitation of service men and women. It is an event that works to inspire recovery and enable those taking part to move beyond their illness and injury. The cynics might argue that it is there to nullify veterans' anger and organise us along 'happy clappy' lines. Either way, it was a turning point in my life.

I was one of 12 wounded, injured and sick British military veterans who came together to sing at the opening ceremony of the games. We were pulled from all three services, across different ranks, regiments and generations. We were linked together by our injuries, some hidden, some clearly visible. Andy was a double amputee who had been blown up in his driveway in Northern Ireland. Paul was blind after he had stumbled across a daisy chain of mines in Afghanistan. Alison struggled to leave her house and Stewart had suffered a severe brain injury. We were thrown together in a series of residential workshops. We each presented our own challenges for Gareth and were a somewhat dysfunctional tribe.

In front of the cameras, we learned to sing and to be together – amongst each other once again. Gareth's style was challenging. On the surface he is immediately likeable, polite and sensitive. His style is effeminate and expressive. There is nothing macho or even remotely sporty or physical about him. The mix with military soldiers was interesting. We were more comfortable with conforming than creating. There is, however, another side to Gareth. He is a hard taskmaster, extremely focused and sometimes intolerant. He drives performance with a perfectionist streak. I really enjoyed working with him. I grew to trust him. I still believe he had our genuine best interests at heart and I think he found the whole production emotionally tough. His sense of responsibility to tell our stories seemed to weigh on him personally. It was the way he built the trust between us that was key – without such a strong connection, I think there were times when many of us would have quit.

Throughout filming, I was terrified I might expose my true emotions and lose control. For years, I had contained any expression. My piano still sat collecting dust and my voice until now had remained silent. It was more than a case of simply not sharing my song with others – there was no expression, even when completely alone. The tears had stopped falling. It was as if there was a blockage, something restraining my freedom to express what I felt inside. I was not even sure that I knew what I felt anymore. My chest tightened and my breathing started to race. I found myself turning from the cameras to hide my pain. I began to swear when talking with the other veterans, knowing full well that it meant the BBC could not use the content. The producers wanted this story to be one of hope and resilience. The required narrative was to rise from the ashes stronger, smarter and more powerful than before. Views that challenged the Armed Forces Covenant or veered from political lines swiftly hit the cutting room floor.

I began to project my usual aggressive defiance in order to push Gareth and the film crew away. But over time, with Gareth's support, the music drew me closer. It started to unearth a more visceral response. At one point I said, 'Hope is the fundamental thing in this whole process, without hope there is no recovery.' My children were my hope and remain so; without them I would not be here today.

Filming was intrusive and persistent, but it was part of the deal. The production crew were as sensitive as they could be within their remit, but at times I simply wanted to run away. At the first meeting when Gareth asked someone to read out the lyrics to a One Direction song, I could feel myself welling up and I could not stop the emotions building inside me. I was desperately trying to hide it, but the cameras started to move towards me and zoom in. It is exposing and makes you vulnerable. Crying on TV is not my thing. When I got up from that scene, I went to the toilet to get away from everybody, but even there you had to keep your microphone on. When I came out the crew were outside the door waiting to interview me.

Working with Gareth was pressurised. The BBC had a tried and tested formula to his shows and we were subjected to their method. He would announce a surprise performance with an audience waiting in an adjacent room. That is hard when you are physically and emotionally challenged or suffer from anxiety. At Somerset House in London, Gareth gathered us together in a semi-circle in the courtyard. He told us we were going to write our own song that would reflect our experiences. We would sing it at the opening ceremony. I felt like laughing; it was such a big ask. Only two of us could read music. Creativity had long been stifled with military restraint.

Then he started to work with us to release our inner expression. Each of us had to introduce ourselves in melody and then in smaller groups we acted out stories, like *Little Red Riding Hood,* using just sound and rhythm, no words. It was my idea of absolute hell. The cameras just made it worse. I reverted to being a small child in the classroom and reluctant to participate. I was disruptive and considered leaving. Gareth encouraged me softly and not just in front of the camera. He came to see me at home. I began to trust him and to believe I could sing again.

Sitting with people who were like me, who understood what I was going through and who were going through similar struggles to my own, gave me permission to let go. With every note I melted, slowly transforming from numb separation to feeling more alive. It scared me, but I wanted it. I needed it. It was as if the harmony could transcend rational logic and words, lifting my soul to a new place. It was as if the rhythm had the power to connect me to a deeper, safer place beyond my guilt and shame. Lost in the music, I gave voice to emotions that I had hidden from public view. It was as if the knot slackened its grip for a moment, to free my soul with a glimpse of a new day.

We composed and recorded our own song, 'Flesh and Blood', to tell our stories as one. It was released by Decca

Records and climbed the charts in a matter of days.
Turning on the radio and hearing myself singing was
surreal. Writing the song was a wonderful experience.
It was magical. Standing in the recording studio with
my headphones on watching Gareth through the glass,
I was able to really connect and express the emotion
behind the words we had written:

> Stepping out to lead the line
> I stare into my brother's eyes
> Sweeping sands, the men behind
> We are made of flesh and blood
> Frozen in the morning light
> An image I don't recognise
> The mirror shows me broken bound
> But I will learn to run again
> Don't turn your eyes away
> And leave me in the dark
> Don't turn your eyes away
> I have been strong
> I have been weak
> And I've had days I could not breathe
> But from the dust
> And through the snow
> We come together now
> Now the walls are closing in
> I can hear the cries begin
> Will I ever make it through
> You take me by the hand again
> I have been strong
> I have been weak

And I've had days I could not breathe
But from the dust
And through the snow
We come together now
But from the dust
And through the snow
We come together now
I will learn to laugh again
To dream again, to hope again
I will learn to walk again
To run again, to fly again
I will learn to live again
To feel again, to love again
I will learn to live again
To feel again, to love again
I have been strong, I have been weak
And I've had days I could not breathe
(I will learn to live again
To feel again, to love again)
But from the dust, and through the snow
We come together
To love again…

The prime-time television documentary was to be exposing – a hard hitting story for those watching from the sofa. Halfway through filming at Somerset House, the BBC acknowledged that some of us were struggling and provided an online therapist to speak with if we wanted to. She expressed concerns about my wellbeing, commenting that it was often the people that appeared strong who were also the most in need. I denied her apprehension, reassuring her that I was coping. But we were an unregulated group of wounded, injured and sick veterans and people's minds were starting to fray.

The pressure built as we boarded the plane that would take us to the stage in Orlando. Here, there was no-one to talk to professionally. No BBC clinical support travelled with us to the USA. Gareth and the crew worked hard to hold us together, but there were uncomfortable pockets of tension as many of us dealt with the building pressure in our preferred and often dysfunctional ways. As expected, I became withdrawn, increasingly intolerant and perfectionist, seeking any means to numb and exhale.

The opening ceremony took place in Champion Stadium in Orlando. It held 7,500 people. The slogan 'I AM' was plastered everywhere. The actor Morgan Freeman stepped up to recite 'Invictus' in his white suit. When he walked onto the stage, he commanded it with an authoritative, distinctive presence. His voice was deep, calming, reassuring somehow. I was drawn in, captivated. It felt like he was speaking to me personally as he read the poem by William Ernest Henley:

> Out of the night that covers me,
> Black as the pit from pole to pole,
> I thank whatever gods may be
> For my unconquerable soul.
> In the fell clutch of circumstance
> I have not winced nor cried aloud.
> Under the bludgeonings of chance
> My head is bloody, but unbowed.

Beyond this place of wrath and tears
Looms but the Horror of the shade,
And yet the menace of the years
Finds and shall find me unafraid.

It matters not how strait the gate,
How charged with punishments the scroll,
I AM the master of my fate,
I AM the captain of my soul.

Then, it was time for the Invictus Choir to sing.

Gareth led us out into the stadium silently. My hands shook as they gripped the microphone, ready to sing the solo in front of Michelle Obama, Prince Harry and George W Bush. I had never felt more exposed. There was no more pretending.

We were warned to remove ourselves from social media as the BBC documentary was about to air. They sat us down and talked through the dangers of trolling and the likely abuse. None of us had seen what was about to be aired and we had each released editing rights to the BBC. The lack of control was terrifying. I was on the other side of the world, vulnerable and afraid.

The first episode aired before the ceremony. Millions of viewers were about to turn on their TV screens. The fear of what they might think of me kept me awake, tossing and turning through the night. Yet what happened next was remarkable and unexpected. There were so many messages of love and support, but the overpowering theme was one of gratitude. Gratitude for breaking the silence and shining a light on the invisible wounds that so many people feel they must hide. Of course, there were also those who chose to be unkind and others who gloated, aloof, from the towers of their perfect lives.

The choir flew back to the UK straight after the opening ceremony and each of us were left to get on with our lives. There was no meaningful support offered from the BBC or from the Invictus Games, as neither organisation was directly responsible for us. We had each exposed some of the most vulnerable chapters in our lives, but now found ourselves alone, trying to forge some sense of routine and normality. It was unsettling.

When I got home, a military wife stopped me in the street to make the point that her husband had been to Kosovo too, but that he was absolutely fine. She continued, proclaiming that he had since completed several more tours of duty and had taken them all in his stride. There was even one former 'teammate' who declared at a dinner party what she had suspected for a while – that I had always been 'unhinged' and a little 'mentally challenged' in her eyes. More disappointing was a closer friend who relayed the discussion that had been had over cheese and wine that night; she had said nothing to defend my reputation, or our friendship, as she had only just moved to the area, and she wanted to be polite.

The prime-time documentary filmed my family, my children and my home through the filter of a privileged and contented rural life. Some viewers presumed to judge my social group, declaring a nice house and car to be immunisation against mental illness, rendering my story fake and compounded by extravagant lies. Those storylines hurt, but my lasting memory is of a lady who approached me in the supermarket one Sunday morning. She apologised for interrupting my shopping, but went on to thank me for sharing my story in such a public way. Her husband, also a military veteran, had watched the documentary and was now seeking help for his trauma. Like many of us, he had felt forced to hide his pain for so many years of his life. She touched my arm and held my gaze with a thank you that helped me stand a little taller. I kept every card and each precious letter to remind me of the positive impact, the difference that our openness made to people's lives.

Orlando welcomed 500 competitors from 14 nations across the world for the Invictus Games. When together, I learned from their stories, each so different and yet with one defining aim. Their hope was contagious, real, determined and unforgettable. Their example was inspiring, moving and compelling amidst life-changing heartbreak and pain. Standing together in front of so many people gave me the freedom to show the world who I am. Being a part of that documentary gave me the chance to stop minimising myself and hiding from public view. People spoke of my transformation, a metamorphosis that rekindled the sparkle behind my eyes. Gareth Malone, the Invictus Choir and the Invictus Games all blessed me with the promise of new meaning, new purpose and the possibility that I might belong again. For a special moment, the falling became the rising. 'Flesh and Blood' gave me back my voice; it allowed me to breathe more deeply. The incredible thing about Invictus was that there was this emotional contagion. Obviously no-one's leg was going to grow back, but there was this positivity, hope and energy we found together as an Invictus community. It was inspiring; I have stayed in touch with some of the choir over the years and met up with Gareth since.

Later that year, in December 2016, the choir was asked to sing at Sports Personality of the Year in the Genting Arena, Birmingham. Most of the performance was pre-recorded, but Gareth asked me to sing the solo live. It was a version of David Bowie's 'Heroes'. We would sing while the tributes were paid to those sporting personalities who had died that year.

In the dress rehearsal, we were formed up at the back of the stage, ready to walk on, when a production firework functioned unexpectedly. I left the stairs and took cover next to the presenter Claire Balding, who looked at me perplexed. A lady came over to apologise for the mistake, but the damage was done. We went straight out to sing, but I was still on edge, unable to relax or truly connect with the performance. I felt slightly removed from myself standing on the stage. I passed Robbie Williams on the way back in.

When the big night finally came, the stadium was full. There were 12,000 people. There were 747,788 votes cast by viewers during the show. Gareth was on the piano and supporting choirs stood behind us. As we walked onto the stage, past the silver-plated trophy, the lights dimmed and the audience turned on the torches on their mobile phones. It looked as if candles had been lit all over the arena, swaying from side to side in the seats. The after party was great fun, sharing relaxed moments together and alongside Great Britain's athletes and performance coaches, many of whom I had worked with in a professional capacity. We danced and partied into the early hours. It would be my last performance with the choir. I said goodbye the next morning. I can't explain my decision rationally; it just felt like the right thing to do for my family and myself. I was pulled to re-focus on my children away from the cameras and to restore some semblance of normality. Without doubt, it was also influenced by Gareth's decision to leave. Nevertheless, I will always be grateful for what we shared together and the new beginning it gave me.

I was first introduced to the charity Help for Heroes during filming for the Invictus Games when two members of staff pushed past the BBC crews, insisting on introducing themselves. Several members of the choir had slipped through the net, serving in campaigns prior to Iraq and Afghanistan when Help for Heroes did not yet exist. The staff took each of our names and contact details. I am forever grateful for their persistence as Help for Heroes has been there since, long after the camera lights have dimmed. They first invited me to the Recovery Centre at Tedworth House after the Invictus Games had finished. I remember standing at the entrance, head bowed, heart beating, struggling to make eye contact. I turned left into the coffee shop and sat down by the window when this lady, Theresa, came towards me beaming the most compassionate smile. We spoke gently

and for the first time in so many years, I felt safe.
For the first time in decades, I didn't have to hide.

13

Poison Arrows

WHILE I WAS working as a consultant in London in 2007–9, I had spoken about leadership lessons from my time in the military, but never mentioned PTSD. After the Invictus Games, I decided to say more.

At the England and Wales Cricket Coaching Conference at St George's Park in Derby, I was a principal speaker in front of 300 people. There was a former Special Air Service (SAS) speaker in the audience who had delivered a workshop the previous day. I had clocked him, terrified of what he might think of what I had to say. I shared the truth of my struggle with searing honesty. He took the time to come and find me afterwards. To my surprise, he held out his hand and thanked me sincerely.

I have continued speaking out. It has been cathartic and forced me to articulate the sense that I have made of things. Appearing on *The High Performance Podcast* with Jake Humphrey and Damian Hughes gave me an opportunity to get my own message across without boundaries. There was no client paying for my services and so I had the freedom to share what I needed to say. When I travelled up to the BT Tower in London to record the episode, I was so nervous that I almost went straight home. Even after all these years, I am still frightened by what people may think of me. It still feels dangerous to speak out, but in a professional space I am learning to stop apologising. It has allowed me to own my story and, over time, more and more people have thanked me. When I first shared my story on social media, even more people got in touch and many have taken the time to write to me.

In 2018, Johnny Mercer, MP for Plymouth, hit the headlines saying that soldiers were 'being swept up in a culture of victim-hood and wrongly self-diagnosing PTSD.' He is himself a veteran and a Sandhurst graduate. His comments got under my skin and I spent weeks pounding the running paths alongside the River Wye. I admired his energy and positive intention to help veterans, but witless tabloid headlines risked sending many of us back underground in shame. Eventually, exhausted from running, I wrote an open letter to him on social media. It gained traction and Mercer invited me to meet with him at the Houses of Parliament. He said that his comments were not directed at people like me, but my broader point seemed to elude him. He asked if I had read his book, written about his experiences in Afghanistan. I hadn't. I tried to explain that I considered some of his comments about PTSD to be unhelpful, but he didn't have time to engage in a more detailed discussion. I understood that, but I was left frustrated and concerned that he wasn't really listening. I failed to influence him. At best, I hope I may have challenged some of his thinking.

Disposing of my anonymity has been akin to sending up a flare. But knowing that I might help others also helps me to regain some confidence. It helps my healing. I continue to receive emails from men and women expressing their support. I keep all the messages I receive, whether it is from people I have worked with or those that I have never met. One gentleman wrote recently to say that I 'had given him the courage to speak up and start his own recovery'. A handwritten letter of just a few lines and yet so powerful. They ignite new purpose within me.

Over time, I have realised that at the heart of what I have needed to say is a story of betrayal by the British Army. I think I will always feel angry – the betrayal has been the worst thing I have experienced professionally or personally and it almost cost me my life. And yet, while nothing will change what has happened or what has been done, I am changing the meaning and significance that they hold. Perhaps my anger will remain indelible, alongside my wounds. But that does not mean that I will allow them to fester; it does not mean that I am unable to move on.

Writing has become a way of cleansing myself of the suppressed feelings that have accumulated in me. At first my sentences were unstructured and ungrammatical, but they helped me release years of pent-up emotion. After the open letter to Johnny Mercer, I started writing more and more.

In October 2020, I posted some of my work on the business platform LinkedIn. There was a positive response and the media picked it up. A version was then published in the *Daily Mail* in December and then on the stories section of *BBC News* for International Women's Day in March 2021. Sharing has helped me to heal, to soothe the painful memories lodged inside my body. Writing has been the most brilliant psychotherapy, acting out the silent rage that I was forced to hide. It has enabled me to describe my distress and discharge an uninhibited scream. It gives me permission to be wildly free.

Revealing my story through my writing and speaking has been unpalatable for some people. Mental illness up close is obtrusive and ugly. But through it all, I am learning to care less about what other people think of me. Publishing my words forces me to emerge from my isolation and accept what has happened. Writing teaches me to reclaim my power, and for that I make no apology. That is not to say that my feelings have disappeared. I still find myself often consumed by the fierce injustice of it all. There are still parts that are too painful to retrieve. The fact is that the experience has laid down permanent pathways deep in my memory – I am compelled to speak out and yet I fear betrayal. I fear the threat of being 'othered' again.

My rage has become more than a feeling; it has shaped who I am, and I am learning to harness its pressure and to better direct its aims. It is a force that drives my questioning curiosity and agitates an urgent need for change. It makes possible the depth of self-reflection and vigilance that inform my perspective today. It allows me to feel my anger and for the first time, I am learning to harness it in a positive way. It gives and it takes, but in moving beyond the illusion that I can simply let it go, I have found my best hope of living alongside it today.

Choosing to be open about my mental health has made me an easy target for those who wish to take advantage of my vulnerability. They dissect who I am, my competence and my capabilities without an anaesthetic. They make the ride more painful, but doing what is safe is rarely the same as doing the right thing. There is indeed a climate of more 'openness' when it comes to conversations about mental health, but there is also hostility. Beyond the marketing slogans, there is still a pervading ignorance that sees fit to diagnose, gossip and prescribe. 'Unstable' and 'unsafe' is what society says about me. I have been called 'crazy', 'psycho' and 'nuts.' I have been tagged unfit to be a mother and unfit to lead. People have cast me out, deeming me unsuited to belong to their tribe. They challenge the truth of my experience behind a fickle veil of compassion. They challenge the validity of my response and their intolerance re-traumatises me each time. Calling someone 'mad' is not a compliment, it is an attack. Calling someone unstable completely dismisses them.

You cannot forget when someone takes the shame that nearly killed you and shares it under your nose. Or what it feels like to be shown clandestine emails written about you, pointing the finger of blame. Nor can you forget the job interview interrogating your mental health or the surprise redundancy following a short period of sick leave. You do not forget what it is like to be frozen out of social circles so the most confusing and broken time in your life also becomes the most isolated. Existing support structures that fracture at the time when you need people the most. These are the events and the feelings I cannot forget because they have made me who I am today. They have shaped how I treat other people and how I let other people treat me. I hate gossip, preferring to have a direct conversation no matter how uncomfortable that might be. I value integrity. When I was at a low point in 2019, I was profoundly moved when Bethan wrote this to her friend and shared it with me:

What has hurt the most is watching people I loved and who I thought loved me in return, turn against my mum. I have heard first-hand trusted friends use her vulnerability against her in an effort to save their egos. But it has been through the darkest times that we have realised who truly has our backs, and in turn those who have the strength to accept us as a whole instead of picking out the parts that suit them. My mum is the strongest person I know. My dad is the strongest person I know. Together, they have managed to emerge from what has threatened them and this family too many times than I'd like to count. Through my mum's journey, I have learned first-hand thousands of lessons I could learn nowhere else. I understand that love born from true acceptance is a love that heals.

The repeated hostility over the years has at times overwhelmed me, forcing me to revisit the failure as my own. To retreat to some character defect, a weakness that is mine. I have come to consider that my openness has been misplaced with some people, that my trust has been ill-conceived. Perhaps I have been blinded by a need to be accepted, a need to have my experience validated in some way.

The stigma surrounding mental illness means that most of us try to recover in silence and in doing so we build huge barriers to finding a new community. As a female veteran, those barriers were compounded by a culture that was sexist to its core. The Army dismissed my lived experience in a space where it was unsafe to speak up. When I was sexually assaulted, I crammed my confusion down deep inside me. To question such things was to question my loyalty. Back then, my desire to be liked and included mattered more than my voice and my sense of self-worth. I refused to tell anyone because what I wanted did not matter. Belonging was what mattered to me. Safety came from conforming, from putting up with things, and denying parts of me. I was a contortionist surviving in an environment that encouraged me to think less of myself. Back then, it was a price that I was willing to pay.

Without realising it, I have spent most of my life believing that I have to hide large parts of who I am in order to be accepted. Years spent striving to be more than, in order to be wanted. My unwillingness to look after my own needs has held me down, perpetuating the same sickness and denying my healing. I was trying to survive without being seen and so much of what I was going through stayed in hiding. Each time I went back into treatment, I became increasingly reluctant to tell anyone. My friends had no idea what I was doing because I could not face explaining it. I could not admit that I was back in therapy and back on medication again. I did not want to tell them because most people do not understand or do not want to know. Instead, I set about trying to please and win approval, perhaps hoping that their endorsement might neutralise the unspeakable truth inside of me.

Today, I see things more clearly. I am tired of the voices who censor me as 'sick', and in doing so stigmatise me further. I have had enough of niceties and polite conversation and enough of catchy marketing slogans declaring it is okay to cry. I have experienced enough judgement to last a lifetime. As a result, I am starting to consider a different reality. I understand that I no longer have to spend time with people that I do not like, even if I have known them for years. I have deleted numbers from my contacts and even moved house to the other side of the country. I am now a woman telling my truth and making space for the things that matter to me. I have realised that I am free to be a version of myself that I have never been before. That I am free to cut off from those people who make me feel less than, those who manipulate my vulnerability to meet their own needs.

Healing never happens in a straight line, but I am slowly learning to strip back the armour one layer at a time. For me, that has meant overthrowing the compulsive achiever. It has meant reframing my trauma to see in my pain some sort of evidence of strength instead of weakness. I can now begin the process of unravelling how I became so damaged, but the tougher job is to reconstruct a sense of myself that is able to thrive. It is one thing to process the memories of trauma, but another to confront the inner void of what's left behind. Perhaps I am still longing for completeness, driven by a fear that those moments in uniform may have been the best that I will ever be. Perhaps there is still a part of me longing for the warrior to emerge triumphant and serve as an inspiration in this wretched space. The reality is that things have not happened quite so neatly. There has been no beginning, middle or end. It continues to be a messy ride.

14

Soothe and Surrender

INVICTUS LINKED ME back to the veteran community, with other wounded, injured and sick veterans, and in 2019 I was invited on a two-week retreat. The focus was on the nutritional, lifestyle and environmental changes required to heal more deeply. We followed a paleo-keto diet that contains no grains or dairy products and is low in carbohydrates, sugar, fruit sugar and root vegetables with additional supplements of Vitamins C, D and B12. Each morning would start with a black coffee, eggs and a syringe full of vitamins. There was no alcohol available and all food was grown and produced on site. We were completely self-sustaining. I struggled in the first few days as I experienced the pounding headache of 'keto-flu', likely exacerbated by alcohol withdrawal, but I started to feel better in the second week. My energy returned with a new clarity. We were taught about the benefits of intermittent fasting and the importance of key supplements, such as magnesium for brain health. They are practices that I still follow today.

As a small group of veterans, we spent the days

repeatedly exposing ourselves to extreme heat in a sauna and extreme cold in the December mountain water. We were taught meditative breathing techniques using the Wim Hof method (which should only be used with clearance from a medical professional). The breathing allowed me to control my gasp reflex, taking control of my body and mind as I entered the freezing water. There is science behind the approach, but for me the research is less important. What I know is how it makes me feel – the cold allows me to focus, it quietens my mind and allows my body to deeply relax afterwards. It has been such a powerful intervention that I now cold dip regularly at home. We have a cold tub outside and an industrial ice machine. I immerse myself up to my chin for a few minutes each time. Before I get out, I plunge under the water completely. The ice on my body offers relief that no pill has ever been able to reach. It has become part of my daily ritual. The cold immersion encourages me to commit my mind and to focus my breathing no matter what else is going on around me. I notice the birds, the trees and the sounds of nature. At night I breathe in the stars above me. It allows me to re-centre and it reduces my anxiety.

A trauma specialist called Mandy Bostwick had read my open letter to MP Johnny Mercer. She called me to arrange a meeting. I remember driving to her home in Hereford and sitting in her front room. We spoke for over an hour together. It was through Mandy that everything changed. She introduced me to a new way of looking at my recovery, advocating a more holistic approach to trauma healing. Mandy recalls:

I first met Gemma in June 2019 – a slim, tall, attractive young lady looking slightly apprehensive, not knowing what to expect. She began to outline her decision to join the military, her time at Sandhurst, operational duty and the difficulties she experienced following deployment and years later. As she sat down, my attention was drawn to her twisted musculoskeletal frame, dysregulated breathing and her reduction in body mass despite such a fitness regime. So, our journey began by discussing the metabolic matrix of trauma and applying this approach to treat both head and body, given both have been connected since the beginning of time.

Mandy introduced me to an osteopath called Sarah Spencer Chapman and I started to experience things differently. Sarah started treating me, using cranial massage, acupuncture and myofascial release. During one of the first treatments, my body started shaking. At first, it was a small, unnoticeable tremor, but it grew to full shaking that I could not control. There is a theory that this is the trauma being released from the physical body. It has happened several times since and made me more interested in the work of people, such as Peter Levine, who believe that trauma is stored in the body as well as the mind and that bodywork can release it. The idea is to return the nervous system to its natural state using techniques such as somatic experiencing. I do not fully grasp the physiology, but I cannot deny what has happened to me on more than one occasion.

Physical bodywork has been incredibly powerful for me and when the shaking starts, I cannot control it. I feel the need to sleep after it has happened. It is like some kind of unconscious deep release.

The trust that I have built with Sarah has been fundamental to my treatment. When she started working with me, my whole system was bombarded with physical pain. It was as if my circuit board had blown all its fuses. Over time, she has taught me to connect my body and brain in a deeply wondrous way. I have learned to notice how I am feeling psychologically and physiologically as a complete human being. Layer after layer needed unravelling, rather like peeling an onion. There have been tears – not associated with fear or distress, but simply tears of release. There were times when I felt outside of my body during treatment, not always comfortable, but always safe. Reassuringly, her dog Sophie would sit perceptively by my feet. Sarah listens, she cares and I trust her implicitly. She has made a profound impact on my health and wellbeing.

The retreat also allowed me to reconnect with others who shared similar experiences to mine. We did not talk about the details of what had happened to each of us, but there was this silent empathetic understanding. I felt accepted. We would walk in the hills and just learn to be in nature. I was urged to slow down, to breathe, to attune and to notice the beauty around me. Years of therapy had focused solely on my thinking, leaving a gaping chasm in the deeper, soulful part of me. In the peace of the mountains, wrapped in the care of this community, I found it slowly awakening again.

God was not mentioned in person, but there was a strong spiritual element to our time together. A focus on something bigger, outside of ourselves, some greater meaning. Call it what you will, but for me it was still a god, not necessarily aligned with any particular tenets of a faith, but still, a greater being looking over me. I didn't feel any anger or blame Him for what had happened. It had simply felt too painful to re-connect, whether through prayer or worship, as it touched a deeper part of me. Tears in church would ignite my shame. My heart had felt fractured and frightened since Kosovo and so it was easier to shut my faith away. But for the first time in years, I started to reconnect with my spirituality.

One afternoon, I was sitting on the hillside alone, meditating and breathing. It started snowing. I stood up with my arms outstretched and lifted my face up to the sky, the fresh snow falling on my skin. Closing my eyes, I started quietly praying. When I came around, the sheep had encircled me amidst the dusty blanket of snow. They formed an almost perfect semi-circle in front of where I was standing. Perhaps it was just feeding time, but it was a moment that felt incredibly special to me. I spent hours seated alone on that hillside during those weeks. It gave me a peace that I had not found for years.

Today, my symptoms have reduced but they are still present, even if most of the time I can control them. I know better than to proclaim myself healed. I still get angry at things that would not trouble most people. I still experience flashbacks and insomnia, and my hyper-vigilance can become incapacitating. The anxiety intrudes with different velocities. It might harass all day without a name, or hijack my senses leaving me trembling, the urge to vomit overwhelming any civility. It feels like a virus that poisons me. It makes my arms and legs so heavy that my chest sinks and I struggle to breathe.

It has been 20 years but the panic still comes at any time of the day and night. When it happens, it creates this distorted world, as if everyone else is speeding up around me. Alone, time stands still as intrusive images consume me; red wellington boots fixed in the sheet of ice. Faces arise from the murky water, dripping mud and white lime. What lies beneath is an imaginary terror that repeats itself time after time. There is no bottom to it. I did not see those faces in that shallow grave, just the red wellington boots and the horror of what the villagers described. I can hear the hollow echo of the man breaking the ice – *knock, knock, knock* – and I can see the pulp and paste swirling under the surface. I fear the smell and sounds that leave me physically sick, confused, startled and terrified.

I am unable to control my reaction as I walk down the street; sounds sometimes startle me. When I go out, I choose a chair that will keep my back to the wall and preferably pushed to the corner. Whenever my daughter and I go for coffee, she knows which table will tick the most boxes and we are now able to laugh together at my eagerness to be antisocial. I clock who arrives, who sits near us and who moves seats. At times, my hyper-vigilance makes my world exhausting, and I tend to plug in my headphones to force some respite.

I find myself declining social invitations, wanting to be alone and out of sight. When I feel overwhelmed, I disappear to the isolation of the mountains for days at a time. I am happiest there.

There are triggers that I can predict and so avoid, but more often it attacks unannounced. There are times when it affects my ability to work unimpeded. In 2017, I was consulting with the England Cricket team, when events suddenly left me lurching. We had just come back from winter training in Dubai and now were on tour in Sri Lanka. One morning, I was walking behind the stadium when this smell, without warning, besieged me. The pungent rubbish left decaying in the sluice catapulted me back to Pristina. I was left gagging and unable to step inside. For weeks, I went without lunch to avoid the trigger, the smell and rotting waste. Unwilling to share what was happening with anyone, I became increasingly avoidant and distant. I returned home exhausted, withdrawn and disinclined to step outside.

When I am triggered, I am pushed beyond my normal zone of tolerance. I was working at a school, lacrosse coaching, sitting in the lunch hall, always in the corner, always able to see everything. Suddenly, a tray and its contents crashed onto the floor beside me. Startled, I took cover, my head in my hands briefly, muttering an involuntary expletive within earshot of those around me. In employment terms, it is easy to judge such behaviour as unprofessional. No-one stops to consider why. Crippling self-doubt distorts each nuance and every detail. When it happens, an aching sadness clouds my burdened mind. It is an expression of the unwanted memories and fears that persist inside of me. I withdraw further away from everyone.

People talk of 'bouncing back' as if it is easy but I would liken it to desperately clawing through thick, sucking sludge. In the Army, resilience was about pushing through some extraordinary feat of endurance. I now understand the misconception – true resilience is about how you recharge not about how you endure. I am learning to accept that 'manning up' with a few more push-ups will not solve everything. I am learning that the resilient military tropes of 'no pain, no gain' do not help me today.

Self-acceptance has been the hardest challenge for which no medication can be prescribed. After all, when you believe that something is shamefully wrong with you, then your need for approval hits overdrive. The real work has been in learning to accept failure and pain, and that brokenness and vulnerability are acceptable. My journey has not been simply about getting over PTSD, it has been to work through the layers of anger and self-hate, discovering that I actually like what is hidden deep down there. It has been easier to self-sabotage and self-destruct but I am learning to fall in love with myself all over again. I am learning a newfound respect for who I am and for who I am becoming.

I am beginning to see things differently, to search deeper, to change more fundamentally, and unlearn many of the lessons that served me so well at the start. I have chosen to give up the image of who I thought I was supposed to be – to recast the go-to hero for a more human, more imperfect script; to shatter the macho myth of invincibility and hold up my imperfections. Within my own darkness, I am learning to welcome the light. It is worth more than my qualifications or the medals gathering dust, and more than the letters after my name. It has required soul-searching and it has made me more vulnerable, but through the discomfort I have found a profound courage that teaches me to show up as I truly am. I am discovering a bravery that shows me the world with piercing clarity, perhaps for the first time.

If things had been easier or played out differently, I may never have discovered the compassion for others that I have found today. The experience has taught me how to love more generously. It has taught me to notice and to appreciate. In retrospect, those terrible, lonely years of breaking apart strike me as perhaps the most sacred. For while I felt entirely cut off from the world, I was never alone. I have been blessed with the enduring love of my husband, our children, and the courageous support of a few loyal friends. It is through their love and patience that I have discovered a purpose to my pain, a sense of meaning that helps me come to terms with the past, and an opportunity to find a new strength worth sharing. In their presence I can express who I am and how I feel, because I am safe. It is only together, with their love, that I am finding out what it means to be human again.

Facing the past, I have had to stop running. Roles that I have played for so long are now becoming obsolete as I put new boundaries in place. Embracing who I am and who I am not, I am starting to cherish sides of me that previously seemed unacceptable or even contradictory. It is showing me the parts of myself that I had forgotten or perhaps refused to see. In dismantling so much of the past I feel more vulnerable than ever, but also more alive.

15

Breathe

COMING TO TERMS with who I am today is an ever-present challenge and I continue to evolve and adapt with new perspectives. I still struggle with it, but I am learning to accept that it does not make me faulty, it does not make me weak, it just makes me human. There has been no Hollywood ending, no full-stop or final chapter, however unsettling that may seem.

As I write this, I am still taking anti-depressants and controlled medication to fight my anxiety. Sometimes, I turn to sleeping pills. It is a work in progress – I cannot wipe the slate clean. When all is well, I am energised by new possibilities, I am inspired by what might be. My story is not something I feel ashamed of anymore, but I still have moments when I grieve for what I lost. There is an impenetrable sadness that bleeds for what could have been. The fact is, it might be #oktosay, but getting meaningful help is not that easy. Effective trauma care involves more than the neck up. It requires more than just pills and talking. We need a holistic approach, taking in the whole body, to help rebalance the person inside. These days, I am much more cautious. Anyone commissioned to look into my mind had better know what they are doing.

When I look back, I see an unrecognisable version of me. But there is no magic pill or button to rewind to the person that I used to be. I continue to grow and to grieve. They say if the trauma does not kill you then it makes you stronger. The truth is that you may see a tough outer skin, but inside I am still fragile and hurting. I am constantly on my guard. I get angry far too easily. I overreact to any situation that threatens me. Trying to control it is simply exhausting. What lies beneath the struggle is too often a simmering rage, poised to unravel me.

I am still learning to take stock of the good that has come from the experience. I am learning to be kind to myself, to be compassionate to me. But I wish I did not have to and that I was not continually exhausted or fearful of the effect I had on others around me. I worry that I will carry this for the rest of my life, but my hope is that I will keep moving forward and I will learn to leave more chapters behind me. No-one is infallible; I am still coming to terms with that. I am still learning to take it in. For years, I have been encouraged to 'let it go' and 'move on' but those words never sit easy. For the moment it feels good to just 'let it be'.

My military service has both strengthened and weakened my resilience. I will always be 545991 Captain Morgan on some level, but that is not who I am, it is just something that I have done with a few years of my life. There is still struggle, but today I choose to live my experience out loud. The pain is not gone

– it lives on in me, but so does the perspective that it has granted me. I cannot change what has happened, but I do have some control over the sense that I make of it. It is not despite, but *because* of my past that I have found new meaning and purpose. And as much as some of it still haunts me, almost everything that I went through, going right to the edge and looking over it, has helped me grow as a mother, as a wife and as a human being. I have learned to value the womanhood that is essential to my being. I have developed the courage to show who I am – vulnerable, courageous and strong all at the same time. Dreams have been lost and some relationships destroyed, but it has forced me to abandon the pretence, to re-examine my beliefs and to reset my priorities. I have learned to choose my friends more wisely. I have stopped pretending just to please people or to fit in with who they need me to be.

I have started to breathe again. I have learned to venture out alone, to leave others behind me. I am finding a way to make the mountains my own, to adventure on my own terms once more. I remember discovering how physically weak I had become, finding it hard to run, to carry any weight without considerable pain. The things that I had been so proud of – being strong, capable and able to look after myself had drifted away. Then two years ago I made a commitment to get fit before my 50th birthday. I am indebted to my friend, trainer and neuromuscular therapist Martin Hall, who has guided my training. I arrived at Martin's gym anticipating the familiar 'no pain, no gain' routine from my army days. But Martin introduced me to a different method, attuning to what my body was trying to tell me. We initially focused on calming certain receptor 'dysfunctions' in my central nervous system which had been subconsciously triggering aberrant 'fight or flight' and pain responses. It was like resetting an oversensitive car alarm. And then, with the majority of the functional neurology work done, we began the strength and conditioning in earnest. Fast forward to now and there are moments when every ageing sinew screams for me to quit, then Martin's frank sincerity pulls me from self-pity. And today I am stronger than I have ever been. My body once again empowers me.

I am back consulting, travelling across the world to help others lead more effectively. Demand for me to speak about the impact of culture on performance and wellbeing is growing. I am privileged to be an ambassador for Help for Heroes and help other wounded, sick and injured veterans today. But perhaps the most amazing thing about this journey is what we have learned together as a family that, without my PTSD, I am not sure we would have discovered. It has blessed us with a compulsion to notice, to appreciate and to love each other unconditionally. The home that we share today is the warmest that it has ever been, and that is something that I am deeply grateful for. My children now laugh with me; we chuckle when I fall out of my seat or take cover in broad daylight. They announce their arrival before entering a room and protect me from the deadly threat of party balloons that make me so uptight. When it happens, my body still flinches, but they accept me – warts and all – and that is something that I will always treasure. My incredible husband has stood by me through everything. David and the kids give me the reason to stay the course and see it through. It is their love that holds me, their strength that melts the demons away. It is their faces, their warmth and their smiles that light up my soul and sustain me. Even through the toughest of moments, they are everything.

There are still times when the stigma cuts so deep that I run back into the darkness and hide. Yet I have felt disconnected for so long that I am compelled to step out from the shadows. I am compelled to stand up and speak out. It is uncomfortable, but finding my voice somehow softens the shame. Invisibility is limiting. My mental illness is invisible, but it is a wound that is a part of me and it ripples from me. I am finding new purpose in shifting the conversation to grow greater awareness and better reflect what living with a mental illness really is. I feel duty-bound to share my story, to challenge preconceptions and raise awareness of an injury that takes so many lives. My hope is that breaking my silence might help another person who is struggling to survive.

People often ask, 'Was it worth it?' and I respond, 'No, absolutely not.' It has been a high price to pay, just to belong to the Brotherhood. But I will no longer entertain this devil. By sharing my truth, I choose to fiercely expose Him.

Some days are still tough and others are harder than they need to be but I don't seek my old life back anymore. I have made deliberate choices about letting go of things that needed to be set free and I am now learning to appreciate the woman I am becoming.

I am left immeasurably grateful for the love of my family. David, Beth, Tom and James, it is for you and with you that I am determined to thrive. If forgiveness means 'to be able to give again,' then I am ready. I understand that it is my duty to honour my legacy. Now, there is nowhere left to hide.

The Metabolic Matrix of Trauma

POST-TRAUMATIC STRESS DISORDER (PTSD) first appeared as a psychiatric disorder in the Diagnostic and Statistical Manual of Mental Disorders (DSM) III in 1980. Since that time there has been ongoing debate regarding its definition, symptom clusters, what represents a traumatic event and whether PTSD exists at all. The most recent version involved an extensive review of the literature with expert advice and focus group discussions before agreeing changes and inclusion in the latest version DSM 5.

However, a significant amount of research published globally for military personnel, veterans including civilian populations has shown PTSD is rooted in a complex cascade of neuropathological and neurometabolic dysregulation, leading to auto immune diseases, such as: irritable bowel syndrome, skin irritations, multiple sclerosis, repeated chest infections, pneumonia, cardiovascular disease, thyroid problems, psoriasis, chronic fatigue syndrome, rheumatoid arthritis, diabetes, asthma and mitochondria to name a few, with changes to DNA sequencing and intergenerational disease progression. PTSD is a syndrome not a disorder.

It demonstrates that merely assessing psychological symptoms of PTSD is futile, given it has a larger biological underpinning than any other mental health disorder. Assessment requires an integrated approach to measure metabolic states of dysregulation and apply a wider eclectic treatment regime to respond and realign a person's unique eco system within. However, the secret of recovery lies in the understanding and interplay of trauma genic states, and the ability to respond with the right treatment at the right time.

Mandy Bostwick MSc, MA, ISSTD
Specialist Trauma Psychotherapist

References

American Psychiatric Association (2022). *Diagnostic and statistical manual of mental disorders: DSM-5 TR* (5th ed.). American Psychiatric Association Publishing.

Bryant, RA, Nickerson, A, Creamer, M, O'Donnell, M, Forbes, D, Galatzer-Levy, I, McFarlane, AC, & Silove, D (2015). 'Trajectory of post-traumatic stress following traumatic injury: 6-year follow-up'. *The British Journal of Psychiatry: the journal of mental science*, 206(5), 417–423.
https://doi.org/10.1192/bjp.bp.114.145516

Corrigan, F.M, & Hull, AM (2014). 'Neglect of the complex: Why psychotherapy for post-traumatic clinical presentations is often ineffective'. *BJPsych Bulletin*, 39(2), 86–89.
https://doi.org/10.1192/pb.bp.114.046995

Friedman, MJ (2003). *Post-traumatic stress disorder: The latest assessment and treatment strategies*. Compact Clinicals.

Groer, MW, Kane, B, Williams, SN, & Duffy, A (2015). 'Relationship of PTSD symptoms with combat exposure, stress, and inflammation in American soldiers'. *Biological Research for Nursing*, 17(3), 303–310.
https://doi.org/10.1177/1099800414544949

Kim, DT, Lee, S, & Yoon, S (2020). 'Inflammation in post-traumatic stress disorder (PTSD): A Review of Potential Correlates of PTSD with Neurological Perspective.' *Antioxidants*, 9(2), Article 107.
https://doi.org/10.3390/antiox9020107

Porges, S (2011). *The Polyvagal Theory: Neurophysiological foundations of emotions, attachment, communication, self-regulation*. WW Norton & Company.

Song, H, Fang, F, Tomasson, G, Arnberg, KF, Mataix-Cols, D, Fernandez de la Cruz, L. Almqvist, C, Fall, K, & Valdimarsdottir, UA (2018). 'Association of stress-related disorders with subsequent autoimmune disease'. *JAMA*, 319(23), 2388–2400.
https://doi.org/10.1001/jama.2018.7028

Help for Heroes

Gemma Morgan is as an Ambassador for
Help for Heroes, helping raise awareness of the
challenges veterans face. She was inspired to take up
this role after being supported by the charity's mental
health team, Hidden Wounds. Before she reached
out, Gemma said staying silent nearly killed her.

This book is the latest shining example of Gemma's
resilience and talents. While every word of the book is
hers, we're very proud to have been a part of
her journey.

If you're a veteran and you're struggling with your
mental health, please don't stay silent.
Get in touch with us today.

https://www.helpforheroes.org.uk/get-help/

PROUDLY SUPPORTING

H■LP for HEROES

Luath Press Limited

committed to publishing well written books worth reading

LUATH PRESS takes its name from Robert Burns, whose little collie Luath (*Gael.*, swift or nimble) tripped up Jean Armour at a wedding and gave him the chance to speak to the woman who was to be his wife and the abiding love of his life. Burns called one of the 'Twa Dogs' Luath after Cuchullin's hunting dog in Ossian's *Fingal*. Luath Press was established in 1981 in the heart of Burns country, and is now based a few steps up the road from Burns' first lodgings on Edinburgh's Royal Mile. Luath offers you distinctive writing with a hint of unexpected pleasures.

Most bookshops in the UK, the US, Canada, Australia, New Zealand and parts of Europe, either carry our books in stock or can order them for you. To order direct from us, please send a £sterling cheque, postal order, international money order or your credit card details (number, address of cardholder and expiry date) to us at the address below. Please add post and packing as follows: UK – £1.00 per delivery address; overseas surface mail – £2.50 per delivery address; overseas airmail – £3.50 for the first book to each delivery address, plus £1.00 for each additional book by airmail to the same address. If your order is a gift, we will happily enclose your card or message at no extra charge.

Luath Press Limited

543/2 Castlehill
The Royal Mile
Edinburgh EH1 2ND
Scotland
Telephone: 0131 225 4326 (24 hours)
Email: sales@luath.co.uk
Website: www.luath.co.uk